After thirty years of friendship, I feel qualified to recommend Tim Pomp and this book. This "life message" of hope has been simmered and seasoned in his passionate heart for years, and now we get to taste the excellent fruit. His words are weighty because he has lived them!

—PAUL PARKER
MOUNTAIN PLAINS REGIONAL SUPERINTENDENT
OPEN BIBLE STANDARD CHURCHES

Tim Pomp's timely new book on hope fills a treasure chest with nuggets of encouragement to live life by. Some books have an important message for the moment or season. This book has a timeless message that will encourage readers for years to come.

—PAUL GAZELKA
BUSINESS OWNER
AUTHOR OF *MARKETPLACE MINISTERS*

"Hope is being totally insignificant, like a caterpillar engaged in a grueling struggle. It brings death to self, multiplying grace, and destiny becomes airborne." Those words capture the life experience and heartbeat of Tim's message in *The Greatest Measure*. This is not dry doctrine from an ecclesiastical ivory tower, but heaven-sent revelation from one who has been crucified with Christ in the trenches and who has persevered to embrace a grand inheritance with the Father. What a fragrant blend of humility and sonship! Expect to discover your own journey in the pages of *The Greatest Measure*. It is a must read.

—JEFF FARMER
PRESIDENT OF OPEN BIBLE CHURCHES

Tim Pomp zeroes in on the often overlooked place that "hope" plays in living a victorious life. While much has been written on the importance of faith and love, the topic of hope is more rarely addressed. Tim does a unique job of blending personal illustrations with practical helps on strengthening one's walk with the Lord. You will not only profit from the practical concepts expressed in these pages, but also will find it to be an interesting and enjoyable read.

—CLARENCE ST. JOHN
MINNESOTA DISTRICT SUPERINTENDENT
ASSEMBLY OF GOD CHURCHES

In *The Greatest Measure* Tim Pomp has blended his personal experiences with practical insight and powerful revelation to give us a book that explores one of our greatest attributes as Christians, the ability to possess hope in our lives. This hope will propel us forward in our faith and in our walk with God. You will be encouraged and challenged as you grasp this message of hope.

—PASTOR MIKE NORTUNE
FORMER NATIONAL YOUTH PASTOR
OPEN BIBLE CHURCH
CURRENT ASSOCIATE PASTOR
WORD OF LIFE CHRISTIAN CENTER
LONE TREE, CO

I am personally acquainted with the author and invite him to share on a regular basis, particularly with the youth at our Minnesota Christian Retreat Camp. Your life will be mightily encouraged and inspired by the contents of this book. Tim minces no words but shares his heart to stimulate your desire to know God more perfectly.

—DR. GERALD DERSTINE
FOUNDER OF GOSPEL CRUSADE
MINISTERIAL FELLOWSHIP
FOUNDER AND CHAIRMAN
STRAWBERRY LAKE CHRISTIAN RETREAT,
BRADENTON, FL

The GREATEST MEASURE

The Incredible, Eternal Quality of

HOPE

TIM POMP

CREATION
HOUSE PRESS
A STRANG COMPANY

Handwritten inscription: CHAIR / PS. 40:1-5 New / New Hope, New Life / Dream / Big / Eph. 3:20

THE GREATEST MEASURE by Tim Pomp
Published by Creation House Press
A Strang Company
600 Rinehart Road
Lake Mary, Florida 32746
www.creationhouse.com

Unless otherwise noted, scripture references are from the New King James Version of the Bible. Copyright © 1979, 1980, 1982 by Thomas Nelson, Inc., publishers. Used by permission.

Scripture quotations marked KJV are from the King James Version of the Bible.

Cover design by Terry Clifton

Library of Congress Control Number: 2004102758
International Standard Book Number: 1-59185-564-0

04 05 06 07 08—987654321
Printed in the United States of America

With deepest appreciation to my wife, Cathy, who helped me define hope, which in part was born through a common thing that can destroy marriages: struggle. Cathy, you are the most perseverant person I know, and because of your root system of purity, and never-ending desire for God's best, the very integrity of this book's purpose is largely to your credit. We have a root system that goes deep, but many times folks only see me. You are a true reason for any success that I possess. I will bow and weep one day as I watch the Master place a crown on your head and say "well done." But until then, here I am to tell the whole world that "you are the greatest!" We were just two stubborn Dutchmen who used that bullheadedness to seek Christ, beat the roar of the toothless lion, and truly grab onto the mane of the Lion of Judah. I love you, Hon, my one solitary rose fashioned from the Rose trampled for us.

Thanks, Tim Jeran and Johanna K., you have been warriors in the battle, and you make up the color, the spice, and the petals of our humble rose.

Thanks to Dad and Mom Pomp. Dad, from your bosom has come the most godly, incredible family I have ever seen; what a patriarch! Dad went home to be with Jesus just before the release of this book. At his memorial, I realized why I have been driven to preach hope. Dad's message was love, and my ultimate goal through this book is to define love and faith's powerful, enduring root system, which I believe is hope. This root system was the legacy that my dad and mom leave to scores of people. Mom, you have read every Christian book on earth. What a heart; what an inspiration! Your faithful, steady, enduring walk with the patriarch was my life example of hope. To Dad and Mom Yonker, you have watched and prayed, believed, and helped us to keep singing our song. Thank you.

In honor of my dad, here is the third verse and chorus of his favorite hopeful song, "The Love of God" by Frederick M. Lehman:

> Could we with ink the ocean fill
> And were the skies of parchment made,
> Were ev'ry stalk on earth a quill
> And ev'ry man a scribe by trade.
> To write the love of God above
> Would drain the ocean dry;
> Nor could the scroll contain the whole
> Tho stretched from sky to sky.
> O love of God how rich and pure!
> How measureless and strong!
> It shall forevermore endure,
> The saints' and angels' song.

Contents

Foreword   *viii*

Introduction: Maturing Through Worship
and Hope   1

1 The Adversaries of Hope   6

2 The Preparation of Hope—Repentance   17

3 The Birth of Hope—God's Presence   26

4 The Author of Hope—The Trinity   45

5 The Progression of Hope—The Pathway
  to a Great Salvation   61

6 The Progression of Hope—
  The Potential of One Called Follower,
  Disciple, Shepherd, King, Priest, Apostle   77

7 Hope Defined   96

8 The Mountain of Hope   104

9 It Is All About Grace   137

FOREWORD

I AM GREATLY HONORED to have been asked to write the foreword for Tim Pomp's first book, *The Greatest Measure*. After thirty-plus years in the ministry, I am filled with great expectations for what God is preparing to do in the body of Christ through a new generation of young men of God. Tim Pomp is one of those young men whom I believe has received great insight and revelation into the Word through a life of consecration, holiness, and hunger for the Word. I believe His insights in this book can revolutionize the lives of many people. It is a "must read" for the mature believer and those who are just beginning their walk with the Lord.

I have always believed hope was visionary, more so than an inferior species of faith. The Word says, "Faith is the substance of things hoped for," so obviously the connection is biblical and essential to accomplishing great works in the kingdom.

What Tim has done in this book is elevate the workings of hope to its proper place in the day-to-day walk of believers. I know that as you take the time to study this revelation, you will understand how powerfully God can work in your life to see your dreams and visions fulfilled. This book, I believe, will help you turn hopelessness into God-given hope.

—DR. TIM BAGWELL, SENIOR PASTOR
WORD OF LIFE CHRISTIAN CENTER

Maturing Through Worship and Hope

I AM A GEM to my heavenly Father and a few others in this life. I would evaluate myself in life, and ministry, as a farmer dealing with seeds, weeds, and harvest. I have, with regularity, rejoiced with abundance, bumper crops of joy, and His precious presence. But the greatest measure of my life, although always in His grasp of love, has been enduring growth, defining parched soil, flooded soil, and nurturing my righteous seed. Would you agree the long and short of life is struggling for balance in a very exaggerated, carnal world? The pinnacle of this life is living in the victory of the cross and trusting in the precious atoning blood of Jesus. Because of Adam's work in the Garden of Eden, it is definitely a struggle more than a cakewalk. I desire to assist you in the battle against the flesh and open up a very unique door full of foundational truths that will bring a transformation into your life.

An intimate talk with Master Jesus several years ago resulted in a change in my life, a new vision, and a change in direction. Since that time, the specific fruit of that change was a revelation of the *hope* of God. If you look closely at the qualities of faith, hope, and love, I believe teaching hope is an element missing in believers today, and therefore, we have *little-faith* Christians. My desire is to show you how the entire kingdom of God pivots on hope and must be motivated by *true worship*!

When Peter said those powerful words to Jesus, "*You are the Christ, the Son of the Living God,*" he did not fully know what he was saying. An excellent example of how the hope process begins would be apostle Peter. His statement recorded in Matthew 16:16, "You are the Christ, the Son of the living God" was profound and incredible, but not yet a revelation to his entire being. Through his relationship with Christ, Peter was ripe with a seed of expectation, hope, and undeveloped faith that inspired him to declare this timeless revelation. Only moments later, after his declaration, Jesus was rebuking Satan from Peter's emotions. (See Matthew 16:23.) The cornerstone of the kingdom—that Jesus is the Christ—becomes real through a process of confessing with your mouth and believing with your heart. By grace through faith is your salvation, and you must agree that you are not a soaring butterfly, but still a caterpillar when you are saved.

Peter did not understand Jesus at the Last Supper when He spoke of his ability to deny Jesus. In the Garden of Gethsemane he fell asleep and then tried to maim a servant of a high priest. He denied Jesus three times, had a pity party, and really could not believe Mary when she said that Christ was indeed raised from the dead. Faith finally

2

became the proof of what Peter *hoped* for when, a couple of months later, his revelation of hope would culminate in preaching to thousands and several mighty exploits. This book is not all about faith, but walking in its makeup, *hope*, until Christ in you births a life of faith.

The majority of Christ's anointed ones (Christians) are frail in faith and short on love because they do not understand hope. Hope is the makeup of faith, and faith is that which pleases God. (See Hebrews 11:1, 6.) According to Romans 5, hope is the shameless preface to love and love is supposed to be our bond of perfection, according to the Book of Colossians. Christ will come back to a bride that is expecting the king, wearing pure spotless garments, because she has been purified in the refiner's fire. He wants a people who are waiting with humility, not gloating with religious robes of status and privately drinking the poison of the deafness of this world. Since I had that encounter with the Master He has defined for me hundreds of synonyms for hope that ignite my life and perspective constantly. More importantly, He has shown me ways to implement that hope.

The parable of the sower is a great way to open your *hope* curiosity. In the movements of faith, many have jumped to the verse that says, "plant your seed on good soil" (Mark 4:8, author's paraphrase), and then add, *and then claim one hundredfold return.* Hallelujah! Amen! Praise the Lord! Exciting teaching, but most people live in its unreality and end up hopeless. I believe the reality of this passage teaches the truth about tribulation and the kingdom. The wayside assembly, the rocks of immaturity, and the thorny soil of worldliness are the places that we will begin throwing most of our seeds. In short, even as a Christian, planting seeds in bad ground is a reality of growth. Good soil and good choices will develop through those trials and failures. You cannot get born again and instantly produce one hundred-fold anymore than a baby can wake up one morning, eat a T-bone steak and eggs, drive to work, and run a corporation. A baby has to go through the process of falling down, getting up, and do the natural thing—grow.

If a mature Christian could be compared to that powerful executive running the corporation, we do not have to explain the tedious details and years of preparation. Hope is set inside of us from God to work with the obstacles and conquer them. A paramount problem with the church today is that it does not know what to do with baby Christians. They are born again, and the next thing you know they are elders, deacons, minstrels, and put in positions of authority. Through *politics*, one classified as novice according to the Word is many times put in a place of authority. Talented novices may produce bigger, better, and more talented people, but also impotence and often church splits. We as leaders must develop babies and let people wait on their ministry. The Lord put Cathy and me in contact with several different denominations, leaders, styles, and sizes in children, youth, and adult venues. My judgments are not related to style, size, and flavor, but my hope and judgment are related to *fruit*, the Lord's measuring stick for us as disciples of Christ. Opinions of style, size, flavor, and church government are as diverse as the place or country in which you live, but the question is always the same—*Are you producing fruit?* Identity is the Father's vision for our life. It is knowing that we are His son or daughter. If I am secure in that, my heart's purpose for exchange will be the catalyst to hope. I believe this book will help you to define that the catalyst to hope will be "exchange" with Father God.

So I asked Him a very intimate question: *Jesus, who am I in this life?* I was poised to hear pastor, or minstrel, or maybe even a prophetic voice to the nations. I will never forget His response and clear voice in my spiritual ears: *You are a minister of hope, my son. You are an artist that I will use to paint word pictures of hope and faith into people's lives.* Now understand, I have trouble drawing a stickman on paper, but He has the most awesome way of articulating His message to me. Even though I may be a pastor to some, a worshiper, a prophetic voice, a mentor, a friend, a dad, or husband, I know I am a minister of hope, with a Holy Spirit degree in the arts. That gives me confidence for the rest of my life. Understand that the heart of this thought is the fact that I am His precious *son*. This book is a prophetic, (prophecy—to edify, exhort, and comfort = *hope)*, trumpet blast to a people who lack identity and growth skills, are frail with religion, spiritually fat, weak, and clothed in spotted garments. This book was not written with the intention of speed-reading. It is packed with nuggets to chew on. These pages will speak to people who focus on position instead of God's purpose, to become a *child*. Every good gift—fivefold, spiritual, and motivational—comes from the Father. Oh how the usage of those gifts have been cursed by man's quest for position and power. No gift of any kind will ever compare with the hope of relationship to Christ. Please pause and think about that statement. Jesus screamed, not at the sinner, but the *religious ones*. Christ's kingdom is not spiritual fast food, or hundred yard dashes. God's pattern, according to Romans 5:1–5, begins with trials which build character and unashamed *hope* and finally a pearl of great price called *love*. Mark these words: hope will make up the greatest measure of your life.

CHAPTER 1

The Adversaries of Hope

FRED, A STATE finalist throughout high school in wrestling, had Coke bottle glasses and an entourage of followers who worshiped the ground he walked on. Exactly why he hated my guts was way beyond my comprehension at that time. Today it is clear that this hard lesson would be foundational in my journey of life. Just walking down the school halls was intimidating, and I would do anything and walk any distance to avoid crossing his path. One time I remember walking into the gym past a stage with an impassable posse of Fred-ites ready for some fun. Piercing me with a knife would have been less painful than the slander with his vulgar words in front of peers. He was just plain vile, and his posture was arrogant and proud like Goliath himself. I can imagine the enemy of my soul, cheering those kairos moments for his kingdom, not knowing that there was a David inside of me that would manifest in the very near future. My legs would get woozy and my stomach would start churning to just look in his direction. It is not like I had lots of friends the way it was, without Stud Fred's antics. He featured in pulling gym shorts to the floor from behind, deadly blows to the shoulder, and powerful, profane, piercing words. There was a period of time that I saw the power of the devil himself revealed through this yielded dark vessel.

The climax of his defiance toward me peaked one day as I was caught alone in a weight room with him. I was facing away as he entered, minding my own business. The episode was quick and thoughtless, and would highlight a defiling moment to a nightmarish chapter in my life. Without warning, he came behind me, and with all his might kicked me very hard directly in the sensitive part of my behind with his pointed cowboy boots. Now he had me where he wanted me. A lonely feeling of hopelessness would hardly explain my grief, as he parted with some more piercing words, *You are a loser, Pomp*. Of course his unspoken words and jeers of victory were also powerful as he left me, lying on the ground writhing in pain. It was interesting how his final act of terrorism came to me without his Fred-ites present. Weeping and hurting and praying to not meet any peers, I hobbled gingerly, a very long three blocks that would take me to the refuge of my bedroom. I still remember plopping down on my bed, contemplating the most terrifying moment of my life.

Anger, hatred, and even thoughts of murder were emotions that were quite foreign to my life. My blessed home and upbringing, and the life of a preacher's kid in the seventies in South Dakota, was far from the divorce courts of the nineties. My very immature walk with God woke up that day as alarms of all kinds were ringing and raging inside of me. It was at a crucial moment in time, as millions before and after me can relate to the *tests of life*. Should I plot my revenge or forget the whole thing, in hopes of never facing him again? I could tell authorities and be guaranteed another episode of *As the Stomach Turns, the preacher's kid meets Freddie Kruger*. But by God's most awesome grace, another scenario surfaced and would prove to be an avenue of hope to my life that continues giving to this day.

Divine would be an understatement in describing the talk I had with Jesus in that moment. I really was in new territory regarding my conscience and the discovery of things like forgiveness, and healing, and talking to God. I promptly directed my on-fire emotions toward the Lord. Inside I screamed at Him and said, *I hurt really bad, and I cannot and will not forgive Freddie.* The Father seemed to say, *Who said anything about forgiveness; I am just listening and want to be with you.* Later in life I would recognize that the Spirit inside me was testifying to the forgiving power of the cross. He does not push forgiveness; its redemptive option just waits for us to draw from it. Oswald Chambers says that redemption has two distinct qualities: it *creates* and it *satisfies*. We will talk about Jesus, our redeemer, in a later chapter.[1]

After battling with Coke bottle glasses and those proverbial cowboy boots, I remember tears rolling from my eyes, pain shooting in my behind parts, and powerful images of all kinds raging before me. Something seemed to take my posture in this teenage nightmare and gently began to turn me around. It is as if I was in a swivel chair, and behind me was a secret treasure. Slowly, with great gentleness, He turned me, as my thoughts still raged of

8

cowboy boots and humiliation. Next, a fantastic thing happened; my eyes were fixed on the cross of Jesus and His pierced body, hands, and feet. Then the words rang through my being, *Father forgive them for they know not what they do.*

Thank the Lord for Sunday school and Easter sermons. Somehow, with no aid of counselors or mentors, the Lord gave me a heart to forgive this enemy of my soul. That was not all. More of Jesus' words manifested in my thoughts: *for they know not what they do.* I divinely understood a simple fact, that Fred did not know what he was doing. I remember imagining myself and Fred in ten years. What would forgiveness, or a life of defiance, create as our destiny? The answer to that was discovered over five years later when I visited and found out that Fred's sports talent took him neither to collegiate or marital success. He was divorced, and I was enjoying an exciting life and building foundations for a life of ministry. I knew I had forgiven him because I felt like weeping when I heard of his ruin. Wherever he is, Jesus, bless him and bring him Your knowledge.

WORLDLY WISDOM

> But if you have bitter envy and self-seeking in your hearts, do not boast and lie against the truth. This wisdom does not descend from above, but is earthly, sensual, demonic. For where envy and self-seeking exist, confusion and every evil thing are there.
> —JAMES 3:14–16

Everyone has had a cowboy boot incident, or something like it, and I am very aware of the divine result to my own experience. The Word says in Hebrews 12:15 that a person like Fred is a root of bitterness that can spring up and defile many. Remember that the makeup of faith is hope and this vein of unforgiveness is huge in extinguishing hope in all facets of life. In my story, I had knowledge of the cross and the fact that I should forgive. Through a surrendering of my will, God's hope grabbed onto my knowledge and converted it to understanding. Of the big three, knowledge (facts, information), wisdom (applied knowledge), and the ultimate goal, understanding is the catalyst and the pivotal act of your will toward wise choices. Think of when you are talking to a child. You do not say, *Are you wise?* or *Do you have knowledge?* You say, *Do you understand?* Regarding bears, lions, and cowboy boots in a life, hope is closely tied to your will. A hopeless Christian is one who denies God's voice when challenged to yield to Satan's traps. Tribulation is the first step in God's kingdom process. Trials and tests are to our life what rain, wind, and storms are to a seedling. James 1:12 declares that the crown of life is rewarded to those who endure, and do not forget that the context of that chapter is godly wisdom. By grace, the Lord rewarded me with forgiveness through understanding instead of bitterness through anger and folly. Proverbs 20:5 says, "Counsel in the heart of man is like deep water, [or a deep well], but a man of understanding will *draw it out.*" "Counsel" represents something in a saint's life that is crucial for growth. Understanding is the bridge in the all important pathway from knowledge to wisdom. So my personal definition of understanding is "the hope of God's counsel." James 3 continues in defining godly wisdom:

> But the wisdom that is from above is first pure, then peaceable, gentle, willing to yield, full of mercy and good fruits, without partiality and without hypocrisy.
> —JAMES 3:17, NKJV

Our ultimate goal in life should be to have godly wisdom, strong faith, and agape love. But knowledge in many cases will only puff-up and become sensual if it fails the test of understanding and gives up before becoming wisdom. (See James 3:15.) If my life was nearing a close, to me it would be short of the best to have on my epitaph, "a man of knowledge." Without the bridge, the catapult, and the process of understanding (the hope of God's counsel), His crown of wisdom in you will not emerge.

Your adversary may be related to sex, drugs, rock-n-roll, financial ruin, anger, bitterness, or religious status. Your counsel may be good, bad, or nonexistent, but the cross of Christ through the Father's heart is the only counsel that will bring the spirit of understanding. (See Ephesians 1:18.) So whatever your adversary may be, remember the power of the cross. The spirit of understanding will be in you and be a vital element as you pursue the true hope of God.

JUDGMENT

> "Judge not, that you be not judged. For with what judgment you judge, you will be judged; and with the measure you use, it will be measured back to you."
> —MATTHEW 7:1–2

My purpose throughout this book is to define hope in the context of worshiping God and to touch other crucial areas that pertain to hope. It seems that in my entire life with Christ, not even a month has gone by without the important principle of judgment coming up somewhere. Whether dealing with marital relations, the flesh, addictions, or any conflict in my life or with others, it seems like Matthew 7:1–2 comes into play. If you are one who tends to make quick judgments that are spoon-sized, that is what will return to you. But many are in trouble because they are making dump truck-sized judgments. Now under the topic of hope's adversaries, judgment is indirectly at the top of the list. Just like this verse, judgment has a boomerang effect; it comes back to bite you. While expressing what seems natural, this incredible principle of judgment seems to uncover true motives. God created you in His image, and, like it or not, the God-authority given to you is powerful. Your words carry dominion and it is up to you to make them positive or negative. A simple example is one who has learned to use curse words and profanity. These words come straight from a place that defines your character. You say, *It does not affect me when a cuss word slips out.* Proverbs 18:21 says, "Death and life are in the power of the tongue, and those who love it will eat its fruit." Also, remember the third commandment: *do not take the name of the Lord thy God in vain, one who does so will not be held guiltless,* (author's paraphrase). There is no greater enemy to your hope than words, or judgments that come from your sin nature. These words are scud missiles of despair that spring back at the most inopportune time. Jesus, at Calvary, and the beloved Stephen, before being stoned to death, had the ultimate answer to the *judgment* problem: "Father, forgive them for they know not what they do." (See Luke 23:34.)

Please define within yourself the places that are ruled by flesh and an evil tongue, and if you judge, judge yourself. What is hopeless? Hopeless is taking the sacrament of communion and damning yourself while eating and drinking because you did not judge yourself. (See 1 Corinthians 11:23–33.) I realize those are tough words, but no sin has power over the cross to those who accept His blood. Allow this blood-bought authority to handle your judgments. James three declares that God's wisdom is *first pure*. The only answer for a life of clouded judgment and walking in that place of folly, is to genuinely partake of the Lord's body and blood. Freedom from judgment is all about the hope of the cross of Jesus.

SHAME

> But we have renounced the hidden things of shame, not walking in craftiness nor handling the word of God deceitfully, but by manifestation of the truth commending ourselves to every man's conscience in the sight of God.
>
> —2 CORINTHIANS 4:2

The topic I am about to uncover may be the most personally sensitive and passionate topic of my life. We all have been ill-affected by the sexual revolution of the 60s, 70s, 80s, and now into the first decade of the twenty-first century. The hourglass of time is losing its sand, and there is no doubt that judgment is coming to the nation and to the house of God. I have been ministering to teenagers for twenty-one years. Romans 5:5 says that God's hope does not disappoint or have shame. What a contrast to the lust, fornication, divorce, and the sick state of the average

American home today. Family and relationships are gifts that the Lord has given us, and we have failed as a nation, and in family units primarily, because of the oldest enemy in human history—shame. Let me draw you a picture. A nice young boy from a Christian home picks up a pretty young girl from his class as they head toward the biggest night in a kid's life, the prom. Today, parents must be convicted big-time in their hearts concerning what they have allowed their children to do. Prom night, and nights related to its purpose in this day and age, define the icon of a very sick society. Written on the heart of this icon is *shame.* You say, *but shame is not bold or aggressive and does not motivate rock-n-roll, or depravity, or substance abuse, and could not be the culprit of this age.* I beg to differ! Shame is ancient and has been powerful since the Garden of Eden when it manifest along with its partner, fear, through disobedience. So the young man finally leaves the dance with a young lady that was motivated by a shame-based music that says, *if it feels good do it,* and *I want to feel the heat with somebody.* Their conscience and possible Christian standards have been defrauded and pushed past lust to a place where they could not possibly fulfill their desires in God. Then we approach my definition of shame. Honoring this precious, beautiful, young lady for whom God created her to be would mean giving her the gift of exchange, and friendship, and talking heart to heart. Instead, he defines his character of shame by *taking away from her* with physical acts that belong to those in a marriage covenant. Let me clearly define here that this takes place way before sexual intercourse.

> How long, O you sons of men, will you turn my glory to shame? How long will you love worthlessness and seek falsehood?
>
> —PSALM 4:2

In my view shame is defined by the inability to communicate, especially from spirit to spirit, but instead, *taking from someone deceitfully because of a lack of courage and strength.* In Genesis what Adam and Eve lost was the glory, or God's presence that surrounded them. Shame selfishly seeks gain with a cloak, a mask, a timid and cowardly disposition that never looks eye-to-eye or face-to-face. I again emphasize that this timidity can have great boldness to fulfill its shameful task. If you define it by the word *defraud* in 1 Thessalonians 4, it is very similar. Now you skim your thoughts over this hopeless MTV society and tell me that this story is not true. The opposite of shame is clear in 1 Thessalonians 4, commending ourselves to every man's conscience in the sight of God.

The metaphors to shame include fig leaves and masks, bondages to a myriad things in this world, but to me the communication curse between man and woman is the biggest hope-stealer of the past century. In order to beat this curse we must live the following verse:

> That the sharing of your faith may become effective by the acknowledgment of every good thing which is in you in Christ Jesus.
>
> —PHILEMON 1:6

Adversaries to hope are as numerous as the blessings of hope. Whether cowboy boots, judgment, shame, or fear, turn your posture toward the cross and hope will fill your soul.

HOPE HIGHLIGHTS

1. The Lord does not push forgiveness; its redemptive option just waits for us to draw on it.

2. The cross is a permanent, hopeful symbol waiting for us to receive from its power, even though we might not understand. Are there any cowboy boot incidents in your life that need to face the cross?

3. A hopeless Christian denies God's voice when challenged to yield to Satan's traps.

4. Wisdom has eight proof tests according to James 3:14–17: purity, peace, gentleness, willing to yield, full of mercy, good fruit, no partiality, and no hypocrisy.

5. The principle of judgment uncovers true motives. Do you have spoon-sized judgments, or dump truck-sized judgments toward people or yourself?

6. Shame partners with disobedience to be a powerful tool against hope.

CHAPTER 2

The Preparation of Hope— Repentance

Or do you despise the riches of His goodness, forbearance, and longsuffering, not knowing that the goodness of God leads you to repentance?
—ROMANS 2:4

As I OPEN doors of hope, you will see that this powerful subject relates to, helps define, and establishes all the foundations to life in Christ. Hope does not represent the goal itself, but the makeup, or process, of the goal. Repentance is a Hebrews 6:1 beginning foundation that opens the door to the kingdom of heaven. Sin is simply the separation of man from God. The Genesis pattern of fear, shame, nakedness, and, shortly thereafter, murder was the first direct, hopeless, God-quencher. But God's way to unclog this dam was blood sacrifice, with the right animal, with consistency, with law, and through a priest. Mankind was sentenced daily to lots of sacrifices until the great sacrifice was made once and for all. "But this Man, after He had offered one sacrifice for sins forever, sat down at the right hand of God." (See Hebrews 10:12.) Today in Christ, repentance is our personal way to consistently, through grace (not law), unclog the dam. Though you may just be a trickle, a fountain is coming. (See John 4:14; Proverbs 14:27.) Though you may be a fountain, a fountain in you can become a stream, and your understanding will soon turn your stream into a brook. (See Psalm 78:16; Proverbs 18:4.) The final result can be *rivers of living water* flowing from your inner being. (See John 7:38.) John the Baptist cried out in Matthew 3:2, "Repent for the kingdom of heaven is at hand!" John the Baptist was proclaimed by Jesus as the greatest born among women. His mission was to prepare the way for Jesus. If we can be like John, preparing our heart for the entrance of the Lord into each area of our lives, godly Christian living is instantly multiplied. John's plea was really simple according to Matthew 3:11: choose the baptism of repentance for your life and as you grow in God, Jesus will baptize you with the Holy Spirit and fire. A trickle one day becomes a river. God's plan is progressive.

Jesus was wise enough at twelve years old to talk with the highest religious leaders and proclaim himself king. Instead, He exemplified humility, readiness, and patience, which defined God's preparation of the human race. He waited until He was thirty years old to begin His ministry. Jesus the Christ, a perfect man, waited for thirty years until being dunked by John the Baptist in the Jordan River. The Holy Spirit was manifest, He was driven into the wilderness to be tempted by Satan for forty more days of fasting, and only then was He ready for His ministry. Let me mention something here. What would churches be like if folks waited until at least age thirty to plunge into fivefold ministry gifts. (See Ephesians 4:12.) What would happen to Satan's strongholds of adultery, hypocrisy, division, fear, doubt, and pride in church leaders if called ones took five extra years preparing like Jesus did? What if each of those same leaders fasted for even ten days before being ordained? What if they fasted forty days from sugar, ice cream, or television? Jesus birthed hope and ministry through practicing His Father's presence constantly for thirty years. Hope grew in Him as He gained complete control over His humanity. He repented of the first Adam's sin, and His divine call soon became the divine chosen one. Repentance is not just turning from blatant sin, but continual freedom from the sin nature. Jesus never sinned or had its nature. He was not only Son of God, but also Son of man. He was tempted in all measures just like us. When He defeated Satan in the wilderness, His hope had matured to such a dimension that He literally birthed the time period of grace. That tremendous hope-filled grace caused His eyes to see the joy of the cross, and the redemption of our Adamic nature through that precious, perfect blood. (See Hebrews 12:2.) And all the people said *amen.*

The nature of repentance is an acknowledgement that you cannot, and He can. That Jesus is, and you absolutely are not, in control. For God's kingdom of hope to manifest in you, you must have a prepared vessel, and John the Baptist's cry to repent is that preparation. I love his statement in Luke 3:8, "Bear fruits worthy of repentance," (author's paraphrase).

19

The Greatest Measure

What are fruits worthy of repentance? John's command here is crucial and, I think, very simple. Have a posture of repentance. From twelve years old, Jesus grew in wisdom, stature, and favor. Those powerful seeds manifest the most fruitful vine in history. Through those years of wisdom, Jesus, in a sense, repented of any potential sin by defining sin clearly. I believe *defining* is a good description of hope. To define is to search out the meaning of something, and if you are expectantly searching, you have the heart of hope. To define means at the end you know the makeup and quality of a thing, right and wrong. Yes, I am also defining wisdom, and Jesus became impenetrable through this pattern of defining and carrying out His hopeful findings. He thus became the truth, and was the master at dividing the word of truth. His ability to sin in the wilderness was simply abolished by applying the word of truth.

Have you ever defined pride in the context of your life? When the Lord dealt with me harshly several years ago regarding pride, I was in front of approximately two hundred people leading worship. In this church, we had a real freedom to pray for one another and allow the Holy Spirit to touch those with needs. At times in the prior months the Lord had given me pictures to share with people that were powerful tools of healing. That day the Lord showed me a picture of a beautiful heart with an ugly spot of cancer on the back of it. The cancer was hidden from almost all who saw this heart. The cancer was a deadly spot or seed of pride that would in time take the life of its host. So I scanned the audience asking the Father to help me find the soul who needed to repent of this pride. Soon my own conscience began to ring, and my conviction mounted, and it was evident that this cancer was on my heart, hidden from almost all who knew me. I went to the altar that day, and I must add, the Lord has not stopped dealing with my pride. What the Lord had me do after that day was to study and put to memory scriptures about pride and humility. You see, the Lord will reveal to us or divide truths for us, but to what extent we gain revelation of that truth is a choice of our will.

> For the word of God is living and powerful, and sharper than any two-edged sword, piercing even to the division of soul and spirit, and of joints and marrow, and is a discerner of the thoughts and intents of the heart.
>
> —HEBREWS 4:12

The sword is a great example of repentance. John the Baptist was a maniac with this sword in his hand. There are three sure reasons that Jesus called John the greatest. The first was shameless obedience to follow through on his call. Next was the camel hair of humility, and coupled with that meek heart was the violent sword of repentance. If you do not have obedience, humility, and repentance defined, you will not have the foundation to be a strong Christian. I have had so much fun over the years with the Greek word for obedience (*hupakoe*), pronounced hoopakuah. It means "to hear attentively; to listen under authority." This is the key to all servants of God, and John the Baptist was hupakoe to the preparation call that was given him. Speaking to both youth and adults, I would like to take a moment and be transparent about youthful lusts. Second Timothy 2:22 says to *flee youthful lusts, but pursue righteousness.* First of all, remember that judgment begins with the one in the mirror. Lust is not just sexual, but can be related to selfish, youthful motives, anger, diet, hobbies, thought life, and past experiences.

Remember that the end of lust is sin, and the end of sin is death. (See James 1:14–16.) With great regret, we must look at the church today and acknowledge that most adults do not have a strong grip on how to be free from youthful lusts. A simple tidbit would be to try fasting three to five days a month. Most people have not even defined what lusts are from a biblical standpoint; nor do they understand that we must abhor and reject them violently, and follow after righteousness. John even categorizes three different kinds of lusts: eyes, flesh, and pride. The lust of the eyes is sensuality, typified by most commercials, billboards, and advertisements in America. Jesus, in one of the Bible's great hyperboles, says to gouge out your eyes if they offend you. You are better off with no eyes and on your way to heaven than to be eaten up by lust. The lust of the flesh is materialism, the opposite of the giving loving servant heart that Christ portrayed. The Greek word for flesh is the word *sarx*, and literally means animal instincts. Everyone understands that our sarx must die, but it is a lifelong battle in doing so.

We must develop extreme theories regarding each lust in our life. Do not debate with people the question of whether masturbation is a sin or not; its quest 90 percent of the time is surrounded by anger or lustful thoughts. Do not even ask me if you can kiss and make out with someone until you are almost walking down the marriage aisle with him or her. No one, in twenty-five years of ministry, has ever been able to prove to me that premarital gratification of any kind is biblical. Pastor, leader, or businessman, do not catch yourself behind a closed door with any opposite sex coworker or client. The Bible says, *abstain from all appearance of evil.* (See 1 Thessalonians 5:22.) Besides repentance, you need Scripture memory and a strong Christian friend or spouse that is fully convicted regarding the above principles. These will all aid in winning against lust.

True repentance has an important threefold meaning. First, there must be an acknowledgment to God that you have done wrong, or missed the mark. Next you must reconcile that situation between you and the offended party. This may be dad, brother, sister, friend, an enemy that is inaccessible, yourself, or the Lord and His commands. According to 1 John 1:7 the key to this cleansing is the blood of Jesus. The final step of true repentance is to turn away from the offensive act or deed. Repentance is obeying the unction from your spirit to turn from those sins that will soon cause depression and fear.

I have learned of a statement that is very applicable here. Depression is a result of a lust that has either been fulfilled or is waiting to be fulfilled. I was ministering on this topic once and someone came to me and said, "I have recently lost a loved one, and You are telling me that I am lusting because I am depressed?" I said, "There sure is a difference between mourning and depression. You have a strong desire to have this person back and now it is your choice to make this negative or positive. You must give them to the Lord." Lust is the first step in the wicked three of James 1:15: lust, sin, and death. You know the pattern. A person, while feeling sorry for himself, lives as a recluse for months, gains fifty pounds, gets sick, and ends up hooked on prescription drugs; the cycle is furious and deadly.

Please do not take me as insensitive, as sorrow, grief,

and mourning are inevitable, and important in each of
our lives. But lust while waiting for a fulfillment of sin
will manifest as depression, fear, and shame. Remember
we are in the context of turning away from sin. In essence,
lust is a perfect opposite of hope as it halts and discour-
ages the pure flow of God toward faith. Hope births faith,
and faith brings forth the bond of perfection—mature
love. When lust conceives it brings forth sin and, at the
end, death. Remember the woman caught in adultery? No
matter how bad you are, Jesus' loving words will forgive,
but do not forget His final words, "Go and sin no more."
You must repent!

The opening verse in this chapter, Romans 2:4, defines
hope. Here's Pomp's amplified translation: through the
process of forbearing people and defining personal circumstances that may seem hopeless, while longsuffering
through each and every paltry task of life, you will not
despise the riches of His kindness and goodness. Instead,
that purging process of hope in your soul will cause you
to *repent*!

HOPE HIGHLIGHTS

1. Repentance is our personal way as Christians,
   because of the cross, to unclog the dam of law
   and sin in our lives.

2. Repentance is not just turning from blatant sin,
   but continual freedom from the sin nature.

3. Christ's kingdom in you must declare that *you
   cannot*, and *He can*, and that *Jesus is*, and *you definitely are not, in control.*

4. To *define* is to search out the meaning of something, which is crucial for an expectant heart of hope.

5. Three sure reasons why John the Baptist was called the great prophet born among women:
   a. His call to obedience
   b. His camel hair of humility
   c. His violent sword of repentance

6. Three categories in which lust manifests itself:
   a. Lust of the eyes
   b. Materialism
   c. Pride

7. Repentance means to:
   a. Admit your wrongdoing.
   b. Reconcile with the offended party.
   c. Turn totally from that act or deed.

8. When hope is conceived it brings forth faith, and the God kind of faith eventually brings forth the bond of perfection, love.

CHAPTER 3

The Birth of Hope—God's Presence

IF DAVID WAS a man after God's own heart, and if the psalms are any indication of God's heart, then I will begin this chapter with a few of many hope scriptures in Psalms. Take a look at words like wait, trust, and expectation and you will see God's heart of hope toward you.

> Why are you cast down, O my soul? And why are you disquieted within me? Hope in God; for I shall yet praise Him, the help of my countenance and my God.
>
> —PSALM 42:11

> My soul, wait silently for God alone, for my expectation is from Him.
>
> —PSALM 62:5

For You are my hope, O LORD GOD; You are my trust from my youth.

—PSALM 71:5

But I will hope continually, and will praise You yet more and more.

—PSALM 71:14

Remember the word to Your servant, upon which You have caused me to hope.

—PSALM 119:49

My soul faints for Your salvation, but I hope in Your word.

—PSALM 119:81

You are my hiding place and my shield; I hope in Your word.

—PSALM 119:114

Uphold me according to Your word, that I may live; and do not let me be ashamed of my hope.

—PSALM 119:116

Lead me in Your truth and teach me, for You are the God of my salvation; on You I wait all the day.

—PSALM 25:5

Let integrity and uprightness preserve me, For I wait for You.

—PSALM 25:21

Wait on the Lord; be of good courage, and He shall strengthen your heart; wait, I say, on the LORD!

—PSALM 27:14

The Greatest Measure

Worship should be the most practical, important word in our life. For me it all began as a teenager who liked to sing. It would be hard to relate any of my blessed life without affirming my dad and mom. Dad was an honored, faithful Reformed Church pastor, and Mom a wonderful pastor's wife. They did not seem to have any troubles with me going over to Paul and Peggy's house for a Bible study. After all, it was better than the many other things a teenage boy could be doing. Now the likelihood of a junior high school teacher asking a young man who majored in mischief to a Bible study was pretty slim, but the Lord saw fit to make her my personal voice teacher, and the rest was history. The first time I showed up at their place, I was so captured by the worship. I was too young in the Lord to make sense of the Bible study, but worship is a universal language. Okay, I liked the popcorn and Pepsi, and nice people, too. A few months later, they would take me to a nearby town to a larger meeting with a room full of worshipers. I was not only hooked, but also called for life to this vocation of worship. A family that loved to sing together also accentuated this love for worship. That night when I experienced something that they called singing in the Spirit, my life was changed, and I would later discover that the Holy Spirit is the doer of the Trinity, the One who truly gives you hope. There is no earthly reason that someone would sing, clap, dance, shout, and kneel in total humility if they did not have hope for something in return. I absolutely know that that something is a relationship with the One who holds the world in the palm of His hand. He is big enough to rule the mighty universe, but has devised a plan to be intimate with each one who would hope in Christ's death and resurrection.

Now understand, the topic of worship is huge in our society. Especially since the rock-n-roll 60s, worship and idolatry toward music have been an anti-Christ that have brought multiple curses to our world. The problem with this worship is that its god is tied to pride, wealth, sex, drugs, and rock-n-roll. This worship has a deadly, evil purpose to it, and is directly tied to Lucifer and his eternal mistake. We do not have to make the same mistake.

> For I know the thoughts that I think toward you, says the LORD, thoughts of peace and not of evil, to give you a future and a hope.
> —JEREMIAH 29:11

Worshiping the true master of the universe will result in a future and a hope. Worshiping Jesus is an exercise of faith. Acts of worship toward an invisible God will only happen by believing that He is and that He rewards those who hopefully, diligently seek Him. (See Hebrews 11:6.) So there is evil worship and good worship and the key is the object of that worship. My point here is that worship, and the faith that you stand in while worshiping, is the ultimate goal. Hope is the exercise toward, the believing in, and the diligent seeking of Him to bring you to worship.

> While we do not look at the things which are seen, but at the things which are not seen. For the things which are seen are temporary, but the things which are not seen are eternal.
> —2 CORINTHIANS 4:18

Average worshipers will always have something tangible and pleasurable to feel, taste, or touch. Their object of affection will always be as the appetite, unfulfilled and pleasure for a season. Romans 8:24 declares, "Hope that is seen is not hope," (author's paraphrase). Is it not interesting that two of the elements that sustain life in the human body, blood and air, are totally unseen by us. So it is with the hope of our great salvation. Picture a dear child of God raising his hands at an altar, expressing worship to his king, a giving and fulfilling that is truly unexplainable. This heart is birthing a pattern called hope and expectation and waiting until faith bursts from it. Compare that with a world where only what is seen and felt is good, such as the lust of the eyes, the lust of the flesh, and the pride of life. James calls it lust, sin, and death.

Let us get a reality check here. I have just defined the two kingdoms, but true worship is in Spirit and in truth. We may be quick to throw stones at others for being sensual and carnal, but what is my problem? One thing is for sure, I will not be a true worshiper if I cannot be truthful before the Lord in worship. If you struggle with judgment it will be hard to worship. I suggest that you return to the chapter on repentance and increase your readiness for birthing. Birthing takes place in the Spirit, not by judging with the arm or your flesh. Let us look at the process toward worship in Psalm 100:

> Enter into His gates with thanksgiving, and into His courts with praise. Be thankful to Him, and bless His name.
>
> —PSALM 100:4

Three levels of progress took place spiritually in the Old Testament. The first was the tangible, physical, outer courts, the gates of thanksgiving, in which anyone could enter. Thanksgiving is a beginning posture, and elementary in one's spiritual walk. Next was the place called the holy place, defined by an act of the will to praise, and where one offers sacrifice. This level includes clapping, singing, and dancing, and sacrifice as an expression of one's soul. Most Christians struggle with expressing themselves from their soul and, as believers, never mature in the wonderful privilege called praise. Hebrews 13:15 exhorts us to praise continually with the fruit of our lips.

This fantastic progression ends with the greatest honor ever bestowed upon man, to enter into the king's very presence in worship. In the Old Testament only priests could enter into this place once a year. There is good news in Hebrews 9:12 when we read that it was not with the blood of goats and calves, but with His own blood He entered the most holy place once for all, having obtained eternal redemption. Christ's blood paid the admission for our eternal access into His very presence. Talk about hope! Hebrews 6:18–19 accentuates this hope and our access:

> That by two immutable things, in which it is impossible for God to lie, we might have strong consolation, who have fled for refuge to lay hold of the hope set before us. This hope we have as an anchor of the soul, both sure and steadfast, and which enters the *Presence behind the veil.*
> —HEBREWS 6:18–19, EMPHASIS ADDED

In order to birth hope and advance in God's kingdom, you must spend time in the most holy place. You say, *But I do not deserve it*, and on and on you go with excuses. If you have received Christ, and believe that He is the Son of

God, you can go to the ultimate place of hope and love at the feet of the Father. As stated in 1 Corinthians 13, there will be three things that will eternally remain: faith, hope, and love. These will be the final destiny, the mature, intimate portrait of God's child. Knowing God's presence is a process that every believer can experience. Do not let fear, shame, and temporary pleasure cut you off from the hope of God's presence.

THE CATALYST TO HOPE—RELATIONSHIP

Exchange

Worship is an intimate, one-dimensional bowing down before your king. Again, the object of this worship could include: our Lord Jesus, or shrines, saints, money, music, and a host of other things of this world. The worship of those other things will have one probable benefit—temporary fulfillment. But worshiping our Lord Jesus means that I get to interact with the Creator of the universe. I hold *exchange with God* first as the most significant privilege ever bestowed upon man, and then family and friends. What do I mean by exchange? I mean we are not robots and puppets, but created in His image with a mouth to talk and a heart to make the God connection. Animals, trees, seas, and all of God's awesome creation were ordained to *give praise*. But His blessed children created in His image are the only ones that can *exchange*. A simple definition of exchange is giving and receiving with someone else. Imagine our families and churches today with a great revelation of "exchange."

> Therefore a man shall leave his father and mother and be joined to his wife, and they shall become one

flesh. And they were both naked, the man and his
wife, and were not ashamed.
—GENESIS 2:24–25

There are many significant things here, but let us start
with leaving father and mother. God's kingdom, from
the beginning, meant leaving or sacrificing the most precious for what would ultimately be better? The Book of
Hebrews is God's message of coming out of bondage,
entering rest, and becoming priests toward God. Did you
know that almost 40 percent of the Book of Hebrews deals
with the subject of the tabernacle? A key word in Hebrews
is the word *better*. A man and woman who are sitting at
the divorce court ready for the gavel to come down have
all of the tools to talk and exchange. But in today's society
sixty or 70 percent of Christians and non-Christians have
passed up this blessing because they could not exchange.
As a result of this void the gavel came down in favor of
divorce. Let me emphasize that some of my best friends
have been divorced.

After leaving Dad and Mom becoming one flesh is
the next step toward relationship. The Old Testament
word for *know*, among other things, means intercourse.
Becoming one flesh, knowing, exchange, and God's presence all seem to be related. It is an insult to our Lord to
join, exchange, and know someone sexually if you are not
one flesh. According to 1 Corinthians 6:18, fornication is
a sin against your physical body. Many times I have been
at an altar dealing with folks who were having marriage
problems and the root problem is identified at a place
where they had premarital sex. This illegal exchange, and
insult to God's covenant of marriage, resulted in an open

door for the enemy. This wedge and demonic foothold results in a lack of ability to exchange. Why is this world so destitute of true relationships? Because there is very little sacrifice, little knowing, and very little exchange. I have discovered a golden nugget that is a powerful tool and gives great revelation to this topic. This nugget is the definition of the word *defraud*.

> That each of you should know how to possess his own vessel in sanctification and honor, not in passion of lust, like the Gentiles who do not know God; that no one should take advantage of and defraud his brother in this matter, because the Lord is the avenger of all such, as we also forewarned you and testified.
> —1 THESSALONIANS 4:4–6

To *defraud* is to cheat, to press like Pharaoh, to get deceitfully, a poisonous hurt, and leading someone to a place where you or they cannot righteously fulfill their desires. Defrauding is cheating others by drawing them into your desires so that they are *unable to righteously fulfill their desire*. Defrauding is cheating yourself by bearing your own light (as Lucifer did) *and being unable to righteously fulfill your desires*. Defrauding is being cheated by Satan and yielding to his schemes so that you are *unable to righteously fulfill your desires*.

Please write down this definition and use it against the enemy. Christians really do not know what they are doing when they stir up their lusts and walk past this line called "defraud." The first thing they are doing is quenching or cutting off heart-to-heart exchange. This soul-seated poison will be characterized by displaying control and manipulation for your own personal gain. The result is leading or tempting yourself or others past a point of righteous thoughts and actions. To defraud is the preface to defilement, which has become an icon in this dark world.

Spirit to spirit

A personal story for me after high school highlights the subject of fraud clearly. All I wanted to do was roller skate with the foxy girl I spotted waltzing around the roller rink. That desire culminated in several months after an intense battle with the flesh. We talked constantly about the Lord and in the weeks ahead I felt proud of speaking my spiritual wisdom into her life. But one time of skating around the rink led to our *going together*, and *going together* eventually led to *breaking up*. These two terms are so unbiblical, and so much of the worldly order, and not heart to heart. Worldly dating directly relates to stuff like *trying it, you will like it*, and *if it feels good, do it*. This girl and I could talk about God, but heart-to-heart exchange we did not have. In essence, exchange is the catalyst to hope.

You show me a hopeless person and I will show you one that is independent, in seclusion, and one having no spirit to spirit exchange. The world's antics will always end up shallow and wanting for more. The word *world* in the gospels is the word *kosmos* (from the Greek) and is defined: cosmetics, cosmopolitan, décor, adorning, beauty, and the regularity of the world order. Live in the world, yes, but do not possess the world order. (See John 17:16.) That principle must be settled in your heart. It did not matter how much this girl and I talked about Jesus, the spirit to spirit was overshadowed by fraud, a soul decision to step over that line of our conscience. In God you do not *go together*, but you exchange heart to heart; and you do not

35

break up, because there is nothing tied, either physically or emotionally, to break. Spirit to spirit is God's way, and you remain friends forever. The awesome grace of the Lord kept us from physical immorality, but it was a painful lesson.

In the context of repentance, to look upon a woman to lust is fornication; so at the end of that deal, even though we did not commit the physical act, I needed to repent of fornication. (See Matthew 5:27–28.) Some who are reading are saying, *Yikes, this is getting a little too honest for me.* Remember, how can you find hope without being truthful? Hope's pathway requires patience, purity, and exchange. May the goal for all our lives be spirit to spirit exchange. I recently married a couple that did not kiss until their wedding day when I said, *You may kiss the bride.* Bobby and Sue had been divorced. In worldly terms, they had no chance for a strong second marriage, but when they met and began to communicate heart to heart, they made a covenant of purity that I have seen only two or three times in my life. The pure in heart will see God. This new couple had the best revelation and exchange that I have ever seen in a courtship. I could not wait to get to those weekly counseling meetings, and I even scheduled extra meetings. The blessed day came, we got through with the wedding vows, and I pulled out a can of breath freshener, sprayed it in their mouths, and watched the birth of *one flesh.* Oh, what a hope! Their foundation was not sensual, selfish, and hurried, but revelation based on God's plan—heart-to-heart talk.

At the very beginning, God and Adam walked and soon the moment of fraud came. Even in perfect communion, the result was fear and shame. Very few take a stand as

Bobby and Sue did, and I have great respect for them.
Yes, they face the same marital challenges as the rest of us,
but if spirit communication can happen first, the rest will
come five hundred times easier.

By the way, I did repent and turn from my decisions
with my foxy friend. The Lord did hook me up with
exactly the right woman, and we did not kiss until after our
engagement to be married. Cathy and I are now enjoying
our twentieth year of exchange. Cathy, I love you dearly!
Thank you, Jesus, for my wonderful wife.

THE EYE OF THE NEEDLE

The scene is the entrance of a city and a camel, after a long
journey, stands loaded with gear and supplies. In front of
this large animal is a small gate called the *eye of a needle*,
which was designed for security and not for a camel's
entrance. Unloading all excess baggage and bowing very
low was the only chance for this animal to enter. So it is
with the kingdom of heaven; we must endure a long journey, daily unload everything that is excess, bow low into an
eternal door designed for worshipers. In the mid-eighties,
I received a cassette tape with a powerful word picture
called *The Eye of the Needle*, by a lady named Charlotte
Baker. For fifteen years, I have been receiving revelation
from this classic description of worship.[1]

THE EYE OF THE NEEDLE— THE GATE OF WORSHIP
By Charlotte Baker

The Ultimate Choice

"I have brought this people together today to make unto you a choice. You can minister unto men...or you can minister unto the King of Glory!" I stood among the sons of men, strong and tall. My heart was filled with enthusiasm. My life was given to the purposes of God. Upon that day, I said to the Lord, "I will do mighty exploits in the name of my God." The Lord came unto me and He said, "What is it, son of man, that thou would have?" I said, "Lord, if I could only be among those who play sweetly upon an instrument and who sing well in the house of the Lord, then I would do great things for my God."

The Lord came to me and He gave unto me the desire of my heart. He let me play and He let me sing. I saw the day when the hearts of men were moved by that thing the Lord had given unto me. After hearts of men were moved, I stood back and I said to myself, "Now I will be content for I have been able to move the hearts of men."

But in my secret hour I bowed my head before my God and said, "Lord, You have given me what I asked for but my heart is heavy. I have a longing for something more." He came again unto me in the night season. He asked me again, "Son of man, ask Me again the thing that thou would have of Me." I said, "Lord I see men bowed by burdens low. I see hearts that are broken. I see sadness and discouragement. Oh give me the power of the spoken

38

word that I might speak the Word and their hearts be delivered." The Lord came unto me and said, "Son of man, I have given thee the things which thou hast desired."

With great joy, I marched before the people of God. In my youth and in my enthusiasm, I spoke the Word and men were delivered. I spoke the Word and their hearts were made whole. I knew what it was to bind up the broken hearted and to pour in the oil of joy replacing their mourning. While men were yet praising Him, glorifying His name, I went back to my secret chamber, I bowed my head in sorrow. I said, "Oh my God, my God, I am not satisfied."

He came again unto me and He said, "Son of man, what is it that thou desireth of Me?" And I said, "Oh my God, give me power in my hands that as You did, I might lay my hands upon the sick and see the healing flow." He said unto me, "It is done as thou has commanded." God healed the sick. I went to the nations of the earth and I saw the sick raised from their beds. I saw pain and suffering go away. I was rejoicing as I went to my secret place. I bowed my head before my God. I said, "Now my God, I will be satisfied for you have given me that which I have desired." No sooner had the words come out of my mouth when the heart within me began to ache and cry. I said, "God, I don't understand. Again my heart is sad. Lord, will You, just one more time, give me the thing I ask of Thee?" He said, "It is done."

"God, I desire to go against principalities and powers, the powers of the wickedness of this world and spiritual darkness in high places. He said, "Surely I give it unto thee. Now go." So I went and the Lord allowed me to go into dens of iniquity, the holes and dives where men hide from the light because of the sin and evil that is upon them. There was a day when I saw demons cry out at the very presence of the power of God that rested on me." Then I went back to my secret place broken. I said, "God, I have asked You for all that I desired and still my heart is not yet satisfied. Nor do I feel that I have touched the thing that You have called me to. In my youth I have expended myself with all the things that my heart had desired."

Then one more time a gracious and loving God visited me in the night season. He said, "Now what is it that thou dost desire?" In brokenness of heart, I bowed before Him and I said, "God, only that thing which You desire to give unto me." He came unto me and said, "Come with Me and I will take you on a journey." He took me past my friends. He took me past those with whom I had come into the house of the Lord. He took me into a desolate place. He caused me to go into a place alone in the wilderness. I said, "Oh my God, what are You doing to me? You have cut me off from those I love." He said, "I take thee to the place where all men must come if their heart's cry is to be fulfilled." At a certain hour, I bowed before a gate that is called...

The Eye of the Needle, The gate of worship! There before the Eye of the Needle I heard the voice of the Lord say, "Bow low." So I bowed lower. He said "Yet lower. Thou does not go low enough." So I went as low as I could possibly go. But I had upon my back my books of learning. I had with me my instruments of music. I had with me my gifts and abilities. He said unto me, "Thou has too much, thou cannot go through this gate." I said, "But God, You have given me these books. You have given me these abilities." He said, "Drop them, or thou dost not go."

So I dropped them. I went through a very small gate that is called The Eye of the Needle. As I went through this gate, I heard the voice of the Lord say, "Now rise to the other side." As I rose, a very strange thing happened to me. You see, the gate which was so small on one side that I must lay aside everything, was now so wide I could not fill it. As I stood in the presence of the Lord I said, "God, what is this thing that You have done unto me, for my soul is now satisfied?" He said, "Thou has come through the gate of worship. Now come up to the circle of the earth and I will show thee a great mystery. I will reveal unto thee the thing that I am doing among the sons of men."

The Spirit of the Lord caught me away. He took me to the circle of the earth, higher than where the eagle flies, beyond where the clouds can rumble, beyond where the sun shines or the moon finds her path. There at the throne of my God, He said, "Look down upon My people."

I saw strange things. I saw my companions gathered around a very small gate that is, "The Eye of the Needle, the gate of worship. I saw them wringing their hands and crying. They were saying one to another, "But God has given us these instruments of war. This sword is my sword and I will work with it against the enemy to bring him down. I cannot go through this gate, for, if I go through this gate, I must put down my sword. God has called me to be a warrior and therefore, I will not do it." And I heard another one say, "Me? Lay down my instruments of music? Lay down all God has given me, just to go through that silly little gate, to be nothing but a bare man who comes out the other side stripped of everything? I cannot do this thing." I saw them as they stood aside in their pride, afraid to bow themselves before a very small gate. Then I saw again, as the Lord brought me closer to the gate. I saw a man bow low, laying down everything that he had. As he came through the very wide gate on the other side, his instruments of music were there. His sword was there. His books were there. The power was there.

The Word of the Lord came to me, "Go now and tell this people before you, I have given unto this people extreme talents and much ability. But I say unto you today, if you do not come through the very small gate, which is the gate of worship, and bow low and lay before Me thine instruments, thy talents, abilities, vision and power, thou shall always be among those who will only be able to minister to the hearts of men, and bless the hearts of men.

But there is a gate open to the church in this hour, a very small gate. And through this gate, only men and women who are worshipers will go. These people will lay their talents before their God. These people will say, "God, we will be Your worshipers." Through that wide gate they will come and they will arise on the other side, not to minister unto men, but to minister unto their God. I have brought you together this day, to make unto you a choice. You can minister unto men and I will cause you to sway the hearts of men with your talent, or, you can go through a very small gate, that is "The Eye of the Needle, the gate of worship, and while making new worshipers, you will minister unto the King of kings and Lord of lords!"

Worship, in essence, defines the difference between Christians and all other religions. Some bow before calves, shrines, works, and a myriad other man-made gates. True and false religion separates at the empty tomb where good works are replaced by resurrected life. The gate of true worship is not something physical at all, but a *kingdom within* that is yielded to, and submitted, by a free choice, to the Master. I feel the church today is on the verge of judgment because this free choice of worship is not being understood, taught, or acted upon. As a result, we have abundance of gifts, structures, and dynasties, but a *body of Christ* unfulfilled, and a Godhead that is grieved and quenched.

Do you see the ironic picture here? God's hands are tied or, maybe more appropriately, His heart is tied, as He is handcuffed within *our dynasties!* The person in the above story was living in a blessed realm of *expectation* (hope), and giving much, while miserable inside. I pray that I have made it clear that hope is not the goal by any means; it is the eternal process towards Christ, the object of our worship. Hope is the vehicle. Passionate love with the Creator and a life of worship is the ultimate goal. Worship, combined with a living expectation and asking for good things by faith, is God's combination. In context to the purpose of this book, faith, hope, and love all reside in that statement. Did you notice that the Lord did not deny this person their good requests? But in this story they were granted instantly. Fulfillment is achieved only when all things, good and bad that we possess, are *freely given*. Added to this sacrifice must be an attitude and posture that honors Christ as Lord. The result is instant fulfillment, and lo and behold, your gifts are there too, to use for His glory.

HOPE HIGHLIGHTS

1. Hope is the exercise toward, the believing in, and diligent seeking of Him to bring you to worship.

2. Birthing through worship takes place in the Spirit and is quenched through the arm of the flesh.

3. Exchange with God, and then each other, may be the most significant privilege given to man.

4. Conception, and birthing, is God's process, but giving and receiving is its only hope.

5. Fraud is being cheated by others, yourself, or Satan so that you are unable to righteously fulfill your desires.

6. A hopeless person is one who is independent, in seclusion, and having no spirit-to-spirit exchange.

7. Fulfillment is achieved only when all things, good and bad that we possess, are freely given to Jesus. Worship, expectation, and living by faith define God's process and combination.

CHAPTER 4

The Author of Hope—The Trinity

HOPE'S EMBRACE—THE FATHER GOD

T O SPEAK OF the Trinity, the Father, Son, and Holy Spirit, and their nature, you must agree that each perfect part confirms an incredible hope! Each one fulfills and bears witness to each other that no other god or religion can touch.

At the mouth of two or three witnesses

The Father's powerful embrace to me begins in humility, as Jesus and the Holy Spirit surround Him all the time. They are not complete without each other. What an example and what a hope from One who spoke the worlds into being. He said in Genesis 1:26, "Let Us create man in Our image, according to Our likeness." This powerful trio was arm-in-arm as they, with joy and laughter, created everything. I am talking about the Daddy, Son, and Holy Spirit laughing their heads off as they stretched a ten-foot long neck on a giraffe. Can you see their creative juices flowing as they made the skunks and hippos, the trees, grass, flowers, bees, and seas? How about standing behind that proverbial bush as Adam saw Eve for the first time, and said woman. God's embrace and holy hug from the beginning was for us not to be alone, but together. He devised a plan, unlike other religions, that no one person should ever take the credit. This God is a jealous God. His nature, unlike any other god or kingdom, is fellowship and intimacy. Now that rocks!

From Deuteronomy 17:6, as Moses dealt with one committing a crime, he said, "He shall not be put to death." Unless the accuser can bring along at least one and sometimes two who saw the crime, God's law says, "Innocent until proven guilty." And you thought our courts made that up. Matthew 18:16 confirms the same principle in confrontation to get a second or third witness. How much more in our lives do we need to build, plant, and establish our lives on the Father's loving confirmation? Years ago, I was studying the high priestly prayer in John 17, and the incredible oneness between the Father and Jesus, and the Lord gave me this poem:

EVEN AS YOU AND I

Protect them holy Father, by the power of Your name so that they can live and be as one, even as You and I are the same, even as You and I. I give them full measure of my joy, even when walking in this life. I have given them Your Word, which the world detests. But Father, they and I are one, even as You and I. My prayer is not to take them away, but protect them from the evil one. They are not of

this world, as I am not, even as You and I. So cleanse
them by Your truth, Father God, and send them to
do my works. By Your truth they will set men free, if
they stay as one by the power of your name, even as
You and I, even as You and I.

Let me quote a few things from my favorite quiet time
author, Oswald Chambers. "Individuality is the hard outer
layer surrounding the inner spiritual life. Individualism
counterfeits spirituality, just as lust counterfeits love.
Personality is the character mark of the inner spiritual
man. Jesus was never an individual, but was always in fellowship with His Father (John 10:30). *I and My Father are
one.* From Lucifer, to Great Babylon, to the rich young
ruler in the New Testament who Jesus confronted, individuality and pride is the issue."

LUCIFER—HOPELESS THROUGH PRIDE

We must abolish pride in our lives. Years ago, at a youth
camp, I remember all the kids being divided up into teams.
One very creative team, who wanted to win the Camp
Olympics that year, called themselves "Us." Their slogan
was, *We as us, we are us, if you're not us, you're them.* Over
and over they would chant, *If you're not us, you're them.* I
laughed so hard, but as the years have gone by, that has
become a powerful principle in life, that my pride and *my
little world* need to bow before Him. Me, myself, I, and us
must all be eliminated from our lives. Today the maga-
zines on the rack include *Us, Me, We, Self, Vanity,* and on
and on the arrogance goes. Look at Satan's powerful dec-
larations at the dawn of pride. Lucifer declared five times,

and God five times prophetically responded. In Isaiah 14:13–15 (paraphrased), Lucifer said:

1. I will ascend into heaven.

2. I will exalt my throne above the stars of God.

3. I will also sit on the mount of the congregation on the farthest sides of the north.

4. I will ascend above the heights of the clouds.

5. I will be like the Most High.

BUT GOD SAID in Isaiah 14:15-20 (paraphrased):

1. You shall be brought down to hell, to the lowest depths of the Pit.

2. You will be a gazing stock; is this not the one who made the earth tremble, who shook kingdoms?

3. You are cast out of your grave like an abominable branch, like the garment of those who are slain, thrust through with a sword,

4. You will go down to the stones of the pit, like a corpse trodden underfoot.

5. You will (be left alone and) not be joined with them in burial.

Wow, what a powerful way to see how Satan's demise culminated. In the same realm as fraud and defilement, pride is an insult to God, and its antics literally describe the hopeless birth of sin. The devil is so alone and deceived, because he has never understood the words embrace and unity. This deceptive, deceitful power comes through perverting God's perfect truth and honor. Do everything you can to mortify me, myself, I, and we are us from your life.

BABYLON—HOPELESS THROUGH DESPISING

God's gifts

In Genesis there was a man named Nimrod, and his gift was simply being a great hunter. In our time, people such as Elvis Presley, Michael Jackson, Michael Jordan, Tiger Woods, Garth Brooks, Britney Spears, and even Billy Graham have become very powerful, obviously for different reasons. They all must give credit where it is due, because judgment day will one day come. If you read history about Nimrod, and the book of Genesis adds some insight, he became very, very powerful. His embrace, both of his gifts from God and his friends, turned into the devil's playground, and eventually he began to engineer the Tower of Babel. God said that their unity and demonic purpose could have reached impossible heights, but their carnal embrace was halted by a plan from God: diverse kinds of tongues. James 3 again is so fitting here, "The wisdom from below is earthly, sensual, devilish, full of confusion and every evil work." Confusion, deception, and hopelessness are such good descriptions of one who does not honor God with their gifts. History reveals that from that spot in Babylon came hundreds of false religions. (See Genesis 11.) Today that spirit lives on as a tower called information, and communication is gaining momentum beyond man's comprehension. The Book of Revelation promises the same fall of Babylon as in Genesis.

We must truly come out of the *kosmos* (world) system, and not be spotted by her filth. As with our current day music and sports gods, I am sure they did not wake up one day and say *I am going to be a god.* Satan's carnal tower of pride twisted God's gift and God's embrace, and thus came Babylon. Man's hopeless, fatherless result was confusion. Ephesians declares that every good gift and every perfect gift comes from the Father of lights. We must embrace the Father of lights and not pervert the gifts He has given by exalting our darkness. I already have expressed my concern for today's church in numerous ways. I will just say that if I needed open heart surgery tomorrow and I saw a computer major in the operating room or rocket scientist with the knife in his hand, the outcome would not be encouraging for me. Gifts and callings that are discovered by Christians absolutely must be seasoned, developed by time, and then used properly. I have visited many churches where an evangelist is trying to pastor, and elders are in positions of power even though they have no business in that office at all. I have seen powerful seasoned servants who are squelched, and powerful gray-haired intercessors with no venue to pray because no one had uncovered and tapped into their gold mine. This breach in the body of Christ reveals that there are two things lacking. The first is making disciples, and the second is waiting on ministry. (See Romans 12.) That is a kind way to say that we have failed to discover and develop people's gifts. So we despise gifts by using them out of the purpose of God. We also deny people's gifts by denying them training. If you are a church leader today, please consider making disciples before building a church.

THE RICH YOUNG RULER—HOPELESS

Through a religious spirit

A young man wanted to embrace the master instead of his riches and confusion. I can be honest with you and say that religion could kill me spiritually more quickly than anything on this earth. If you read Mark 10:17–30, you will see that the first thing that this gentleman did is kneel down and get his Sunday trousers all dirty. Now if that did not impress Jesus, nothing would. Jesus burst his ego bubble quickly and in essence said, "You know the Ten Commandments, and you go to church, but you do not know My Father, you know riches. If you want to grow up and be mature, go and sell everything, give to the poor, and follow me." In essence, pick up your gifts, I will give you My character and My cross, and then you must embrace Me.

I once had a vision that I believe is very appropriate here. I was speaking at a camp with a man who should be serving life in prison. He has a miraculous story. He and his wife now pastor and travel internationally, setting the captives free. He has the ultimate story of hope and restoration. I was sitting in a session listening to them and scratching my head, wondering how those tattoos could translate into true ministry. Understand, I have been a youth pastor for eighteen years and I have seen just about everything, but the Father wanted to embrace something in me. Instantly, my eyes opened and I saw the crucifixion and the two thieves on either side. In the vision I realized that this man was on one side (as a thief). To my utter horror, there, on the other side, was me, all dressed up in a Sunday suit and tie. Of course this other guy belongs there, but I, I have never even had a temporary tattoo before. The heart-piercing story unfolded as I opened up my big mouth and said, "If you are the Christ, save yourself, and us."

Those words were so coarse, temporary, foolish, and arrogant to Jesus who was taking the sin of the world on His shoulders. As I sat there, I was already weeping and devastated at my folly. It got worse as he turned over to me and said with piercing words, "You fool. Do not you even fear God? This man has done nothing wrong." Then he glanced at Jesus, and, with tattoos and a leather jacket and an absolutely pure heart, he declared something very simple, "Remember me!" Jesus said, "Today you will be with me in Paradise." Where did that leave the holy, tattoo-less, nicely robed, religious guy on the other side? My Sunday suit did not help, and my scripture knowledge did not impress Him. The Word declares that some even prophesied in Jesus' name and their end was still doom. Good, bad, or ugly, Jesus simply wants to know us. Forget the suit and do not get all hung up about the tattoos and earrings. As you go to the story in Luke 23:39–43 the conviction is worse. Verse thirty-nine says the thief was blaspheming as he spoke the words, "save yourself."

That week, my repentance was great, and the Father's embrace to me was significant for a lifetime. God magnified my pride through that powerful embrace called *The Eyes of Understanding* (The Hope—God's Counsel). I have spent a great deal of time in Matthew 23, where Jesus highlights many woes and rebukes, not to sinners and scorners, but to the religious bigots like me who need lots of purging. That pastor and his wife became my friends. My blessed dad and mom have blessed me with an incredibly warm embrace in my life. But the Father I believe is saying to you, "No matter if You are secure with a daddy's love, or an orphan who never knew your dad, if you are bad to the bone with sin, or wrapped in robes of religious pride, My nature of love and My embrace of hope will always be available for My children." If you are a rich young ruler, please take off your robe, turn your entire posture toward God's riches, and embrace Him.

HOPE'S REDEEMER—JESUS, THE CHRIST

Are you catching on to this thing called hope? So far we have defined the Father as One with arms open to embrace us wherever we are. To talk about Jesus as our hope is like counting grains of sand on the beach. His redeeming qualities are endless. How often do we make a marquee of faith and pass over the process of Him being the author and finisher of it. (See Hebrews 12:2.) Allow me to pull a few grains of sand from Isaiah 61.

> The Spirit of the Lord GOD *is upon Me* [Jesus], because the LORD has *anointed* Me to preach *good tidings* to the poor; He has sent Me to *heal* the brokenhearted, to *proclaim liberty* to the captives, and the *opening of the prison* to those who are bound; to proclaim the *acceptable year of the LORD*, and the *day of vengeance* of our God; to *comfort* all who mourn, to *console* those who mourn in Zion, to *give them beauty* for ashes, the *oil of joy* for mourning, the *garment of praise* for the spirit of heaviness; that they may be called *trees of righteousness*, the *planting of the LORD*, that He may be glorified.
> —ISAIAH 61:1–3, EMPHASIS ADDED

This was Jesus' vision statement, and why should not it be ours? The poor, the broken, the captives, and the prisoners will be free. Joy and praise will replace the heavy spirit of the world. Notice italicized words in those verses describe *hope, hope, hope, hope*. I am not saying that the motivation will not be love, and that faith will not be what pleases Him, because that is in the Bible. But Jesus possessed the anointing, and healing, and keys to prison, because He *waited*, and *defined*, and *formed* His Father's kingdom inside Him for thirty years before this vision poured through Him. I am not saying that Jesus could not have manifest *Christ's anointing and miracles* at age thirteen; it just is not the way God's kingdom works. So the miracles came, and His kingdom, after age thirty. But redemption was Jesus' ultimate purpose. *Strong's Concordance* says of redemption, "A release secured by the payment of a ransom, deliverance, setting free."[1] As you scope this world, do people not cry out of their bondage, *"I want to be free"*?

I will not forget hunting antelope in Wyoming several years ago. I was mentoring a friend who had a history of alcohol and drug abuse. We got up two hours before the crack of dawn and headed toward our spot. He actually had several weeks of sobriety. We were approaching a reality of freedom in his life after much hard work. I also remember that man was a worshiper. For two and a half solid hours we sang, harmonized, quoted scripture, and nearly brought the glory cloud down in that truck. The day went excellently, as we bagged our game and got back to town by mid-afternoon. We prayed, and I was encouraged by his progress and inspiration to me on that fine day. Later that night I got a call from his wife that he had not arrived home yet. I told her we had been home for hours and we quickly put the pieces together. My friend, after a day of passion for Jesus, singing and quoting scripture, promptly went and got drunk as a skunk and Lord knows what else.

That day to me became a great example of the power of bondage. It destroyed his marriage, his liver, and his brain cells; and only God knows where he is today. Are you bound? Are you depressed? Have you defined what happens when you are depressed and how you got there? Remember, depression is either a lust that has been fulfilled or one waiting to be fulfilled. Instead of receiving Jesus and His paid-for redemption in each situation, you choose me, myself, and I. You refuse to yield your will to His precious blood, and the result is *depression*. After that will come *oppression*, or a consistent torment from the flesh, and darkness, independence, and pride will be your friends. Finally; even Christians can become *obsessed with the life in the flesh*; the Spirit is quenched deep into your will. For people that are obsessed by things, and even for non-Christians that are demon-possessed, redemption's power is still stronger than its grip. I have found that some people's freedom begins with their willingness to define their sin. Get free through the powerful redeeming blood of the Lamb. And remember, being *redeemed* by the blood of the Lamb Jesus Christ is your only hope in this otherwise depressing world.

HOPE'S PROMISE—THE HOLY SPIRIT

Therefore being exalted to the right hand of God, and having received from the Father the promise of the Holy Spirit, He poured out this which you now see and hear.

—ACTS 2:33

55

At a camp when I was about eleven years old, I began a friendship with a person I will call Jon. In the next five years Jon and I spent many hours in the red barn at his farmhouse with a basketball hoop and plenty of questions about Christianity. Jon was my first real friend, and as we learned about God and the Bible, an incredible lesson was in store for me regarding the person of the Holy Spirit. No matter what religion, denominations, and even some charismatic circles have done to pervert Him, Jesus sent the promise to abide in us. So Jon and I walked together, defining and desiring to know God. He often attended a different church, and I had some suspicions about what he was learning.

As we reached our mid-teens, we got into some discussions about the Holy Spirit, and this church had told him that the gifts of the Holy Spirit were not for today. I really did not know, but I would argue that if that were true we should probably throw out Acts, Corinthians, and much of the epistles. Time went on and we were asked by our church to testify at a conference out of town called Lay Witness Mission. That weekend he stood up and testified of his love for God. He shared some scripture and he did a great job. But an incredible moment took place in the car on the way home. He glanced over at me in the backseat and said, "Either you stop talking about that Holy Spirit stuff, or we are no longer friends." I was crushed and confused, and in the days and months to follow I lost a friend.

Now I knew very little about the Holy Spirit, and the way I see it today is that my friend drank some poison regarding this precious promise, and he never recovered. I simply kept baby stepping my way out of teenage rebellion, and in the next year, my dad, the Reformed Church preacher, my whole family, and I received the baptism of the Holy Spirit. (See Acts 19:2.) If you have never experienced it, read the Book of Acts. While worshiping and hungry for God, we simply jumped off the riverbank of worship into the river. Jon and I hardly talked since that moment in that car.

I am sure you are waiting for a happy ending here, but that is not the case. The next summer we moved away, and in the fall I answered a phone call that I will never forget. It was the pastor of our former church. He gave me the message that Jon had gone into a cemetery and, with a shotgun, tragically ended his life. As I hung up the phone, I was struck for life with a revelation of two things. First, the Holy Spirit is precious and sensitive and must be incredibly important. Second, this promise from the Father is the way to secrets and the deep things in God, and the key to maturity. If I seem passionate about this hope thing, it came absolutely from the person of the Holy Spirit. He is hope's promise. I am so thankful neither I nor my family drank that cup of poison! Instead, we discovered that His delivering power rests in the unity of the Father, Son, and:

> However, when He, the Spirit of truth, has come, He will guide you into all truth; for He will not speak on His own authority, but whatever He hears He will speak; and He will tell you things to come. He will glorify me, for He will take of what is Mine and declare it to you.
>
> —JOHN 16:13–14

The person of the Holy Spirit was directly sent to us from Jesus as the agent of hope. His characteristics include: comforter, strengthener, standby, advocate, lawyer, and the one who manifests the Father's gifts and fruits. To build a doctrine that takes away the Spirit, or declares that His gifts are gone, is poisonous and satanic. I also will strongly add that without balance, I have seen the gifts of the Holy Spirit become a great curse to the body of Christ! Under the topic of *charismatic*, churches, and oftentimes ministers, insult the Holy Spirit by not using a balance of gifts and fruits. I could share in detail here, but I will just paraphrase 1 Corinthians 13:1–2: "Without love, prophecy, and gifts are like a hollow, clanging cymbal with no purpose." Read Acts 5:1–11 and see what happened to Ananias and Sapphira when tempting and lying to the Holy Spirit. If you want the deep things of God, truth, counsel, insight, Lordship, it will come through the person of the Holy Spirit. But please be serious about it! I believe the following is one of the most striking and telling scriptures for today's believers:

> Therefore I make known to you that no one speaking by the Spirit of God calls Jesus accursed, and no one can say that Jesus is Lord except by the Holy Spirit.
>
> —1 CORINTHIANS 12:3

Ultimately, what is more significant for a Christian than understanding the lordship of Jesus? The difference between a baby Christian and a mature one is a person that has allowed Christ to become Lord. This verse tells us that the Holy Spirit is the messenger that brings lordship. As I have mentioned my passion for maturity in the body of Christ, please consider always honoring the Holy Spirit and His character if you want to grow in Christ.

Have you ever noticed that Jesus said the *power* would come after you receive the Holy Spirit? The ability to effectively fulfill the Great Commission comes after the baptism of the Holy Spirit. (See Acts 1:8.) Do not deny that truth. It is the Word of God. My friend and I were getting hungry, and when presented with sacrifice and Jesus being Lord, the true battle with principalities and powers began. Truthfully, I was tempted to run with him and be rebellious, but I was not tempted to rip out Acts and Corinthians. I had a great respect for the Word of God and my parents. I believe that saved me from some tragic decisions.

The Holy Spirit seals our heart when we are saved. (See Ephesians 1:13; 4:30.) It is simply our choice to be submerged (baptized) in Him or not. Hope-filled words that directly relate to the Holy Spirit are as follows: fruits, gifts, power, lordship, our promise, effectiveness, comforter, strengthener, and the One who seals our heart. Let us close this thought with another hope-filled promise:

> But the Helper, the Holy Spirit, whom the Father will send in My name, He will teach you all things, and bring to your remembrance all things that I said to you. Peace I leave with you, My peace I give to you; not as the world gives do I give to you. Let not your heart be troubled, neither let it be afraid.
> —JOHN 14:26–27

HOPE HIGHLIGHTS

1. Individualism counterfeits spirituality. Jesus was never an individual, but was always in fellowship with His Father.

2. Three powerful enemies of the Father's embrace:
   a. Hopelessness through pride
   b. Hopelessness through despising God's gifts
   c. Hopelessness through a religious spirit

3. Jesus possesses the anointing, healing keys to prison because He hoped, waited, defined, and formed His Father's kingdom inside Himself for thirty years.

4. The Holy Spirit is a precious, sensitive comforter, strengthener, standby, and promise. He is the way to secrets, deep things of God, and spiritual maturity.

5. Look at hope synonyms in Isaiah 61:1–3. The Spirit is upon you to anoint; bring good tidings to the poor; bring healing; proclaim liberty; open prisons; proclaim the year of the Lord; comfort; console; give beauty, oil, garments of praise; and make you planters and trees of righteousness.

6. Christ's redemption creates and satisfies, and gives hope.

CHAPTER 5

The Progression of Hope—The Pathway to a Great Salvation

First the blade, then the head, after that the full grain in the head.

—MARK 4:28

L ET US MODEL my strategy for understanding hope in this chapter. We start with a seed. Isaiah 46:10 says, "Declaring the end from the beginning." Remember that hope that is seen is not hope. So inside the capsule of a tiny seed, even though you cannot see it, is the completion of the full-ripened fruit. Actually, inside that seed is a field full of potential. The Lord designed all life with design inside itself, so that even when it reaches its final goal, fruit, the process can start all over again with the seeds contained inside. The essence of absolute hope is the ability to endure when the status quo is to give up. A seed dies, and through death comes God's first kingdom principle: life springs forth out of death. Soon a tiny blade peeks out into a vicious world. Everyone, according to Romans 12, is given a measure of faith. Faith is born in you at salvation, which contains seeds of hope and the makeup of faith. Actually, those who press through to produce ripened fruit in the church are very few! These rare people are those who nurture their seeds of hope to the point of mature faith fruits.

Remember the parable in Matthew 20:16 of those going to work in the vineyard all hours of the day. Each one has agreed to be paid the same price, but by the end of the day some that worked several more hours than others with the same pay have real complaints. The purpose of the story is driven home fast with Jesus' incredible one phrase conclusion, "Many are called, but few are chosen." Most have the ability, but few use that ability. Very few have the attitude and determination to press through and produce ripened fruit, regardless of circumstances. Remember, complaining and hardness of heart was a forty year curse to the children of Israel. Hardness of heart quite aptly describes barren seeds. Process, process! We must understand that God sets up our lives to start small, or infant, and end up with maximum potential, or in Jesus' words, *perfect*. Please walk with me through the process of one called into this great salvation.

CONVERSION, SALVATION, BORN AGAIN, AND SPIRIT BAPTIZED

Conversion
In Acts 26, we see the beginning moments of one who

would be a giant for God and eventually be instrumental in writing much of the New Testament. In brief, he murdered Christians and was bad to the bone in his religious hypocrisy. Of course, we are talking about the apostle Paul. As we unfold this God-process toward maturity, you should be able to define exactly where you are. Let us begin at conversion. The following scripture is actually Jesus explaining to His new convert, Saul (who would later be Paul) his new vision for life and ministry. This verse also contains what I see as *the key to conversion.*

> To open their eyes, in order to turn them from darkness to light, and from the power of Satan to God, that they may receive forgiveness of sins and an inheritance among those who are sanctified by faith in Me.
>
> —ACTS 26:18

Let us set the scenario. Saul, the Christian-killer, has just been knocked off his horse, struck blind, and Jesus gives the great vision of hope; *you will open people's eyes and turn them from darkness to light.* This is so typical of the way God works, so spontaneous and unconventional, and it simply makes no sense. Can you see the local newspaper, *A blind guy to open eyes and give light in darkness?* He takes the foolish things to confound the wise. As we walk through the first door of Christendom, conversion, let us unveil the key; it is walking from darkness to light. The New Testament is filled with revelation of this simple principle, and this really is our purpose as Christians. I do not believe it is taught enough.

> No one can come to Me unless the Father who sent
> Me draws him [and, I will add, draws him from the
> darkness to the light].
>
> —JOHN 6:44

> And the light shines in the darkness, and the dark-
> ness did not comprehend it.
>
> —JOHN 1:5

When you were in the dark, you did not understand.
You were as every other heathen, living your life and waiting for the Father to draw you to a place where you could
get knocked off your proverbial horse.

> But you are a chosen generation, a royal priesthood,
> a holy nation, His own special people, that you may
> proclaim the praises of Him who called you out of
> darkness into His marvelous light.
>
> —1 PETER 2:9

All have sinned, and all must pass through Jesus from
a place called darkness into His marvelous light. Again
this principle is elementary, and throughout your life you
must learn to divide soul and spirit, light and dark, good
and bad, thoughts and intents. (See Hebrews 4:12.) I dis-
tinctly remember flashes of conviction and drawing from
the Father when I was young. Once, at about eight or nine
years old, we had seen a movie about the end times called
A Thief in the Night. I stared at the stars that night and
just wept as an awakening process was happening to me.
Other stirring moments were gospel crusades, camps, and
times when I felt the Spirit's conviction after childish sins.
Later we will discover in 2 Peter what I call the *Mountain*

of Hope. When we begin this journey of faith in Christ, He will add to us something called *virtue.* Virtue defined is separation of light from darkness. Every believer, from the beginning, must define all other *gods* and become separate from them. Along with this drawing from the Father will come conviction of sin and will bring us to God's first step, conversion. The key is walking from a place called darkness to a place called light.

Conversion to salvation

As you can see, I am breaking down each process in our great salvation. Please note I am not giving a pattern of what always happens, as each salvation experience is different. However in a biblical format, it seems to me that there are four plateaus and each have its own distinction. My purpose here is in the context of hope. I desire for you to define exactly where you are in Christ. Your job is to hope, yearn, and expect to go further in Him.

> For with the heart one believes unto righteousness, and
> with the mouth confession is made unto salvation.
> —ROMANS 10:10

Speaking of process I believe, regarding a New Testament Christian walk, there is no more powerful scripture than this. Salvation's key is that no matter what part of it you are enduring, you must *believe in your heart, and confess with your mouth.* The essence of Christianity is believing something that you *cannot* see. Acts 4:12 confirms that this process comes only through one name, Jesus Christ. Do not ever forget that it is not just God, or the "Good Buddy upstairs"; it is Jesus, and Him only who has given us this great salvation. I would like to insert a progression of maturity that I received from the Dutch Sheets book, *The River of God*. To grow in Christ, I have found it extremely helpful to find *scriptural identity* for Christians at all levels. It is interesting that in one place the Word calls new babies carnal Christians. (See 1 Corinthians 3:1.) The greek word for this new believer is *napios*, or a *babe in Christ*. Everyone knows that this is a crucial time in one's walk with Christ, and this person cannot live on his own. This person must be fed and changed by someone else and is one who desires the sincere milk of the Word.

Carnal seems to be a harsh word, but the Bible uses it and all can relate to the fact that, though we are new in our spirit, our lifestyle is waiting to transform from the old man. In 1 John 2:18, John refers to his students as *little children*. The Greek word is *paidion*, and represents the stage between a baby and a teenager, or a *toddler*. The toddler is inquisitive, impressionable, and much of the structure of a spiritual life hinges on the foundations laid here. Habits of Word, prayer, and fellowship are gained or lost as a spiritual toddler. The next stage is the spiritual teenage years, which is in the Greek word *teknon*. (See John 13:33.) I have come up with my own definition for this stage. A *teknon* is one who has all of the capabilities to reproduce spiritually, but does not have the wisdom. This is quite true, naturally and spiritually. I will stake my life in defending and believing that teens are the hope of our future. A teen is either testing manhood or is in the process of becoming a lady. David was a teen, physically, and probably spiritually when he met the lion and the bear all alone out in the pasture. Trials and tests become the character builders to determine our outcome.

Many years ago, I found myself in a very significant

learning experience. It was a youth camp setting, and I received a last minute invitation to speak at a morning workshop. I was excited, but in the middle of the night prior to my first youth camp sermon, I was totally terrified. Give me a guitar and a microphone, no problem, but the Lord knew my future and wanted to make eternally clear to me the awesome responsibility of preaching. I may have slept an hour that night, and I prayed for seven. I tossed and turned, and though I was full of God's Word and truly excited to do what comes naturally, talk to teenagers, the lack of preparation and level of pressure was too much.

In the progression of hope I had nowhere to go but up. A few hours later I approached the podium and passed up the wisdom of an opening song as I gazed over at my guitar. It could not have hurt, as I would encounter one of the most embarrassing moments of my life. I opened up the Word and read a scripture. I looked up and said fifteen to twenty introductory words. I then looked down and read the same scripture again. I looked up again and felt a possible dash of courage to begin my thought process, until my eyes locked with the district superintendent in the back of the room with a red face and arms firmly crossed. I am sure he was just sunburned or something, but mercy me, his vibes seemed to penetrate right to where I was standing. This was one of the very few persons on earth that I for some reason did not like very much. In the significant moments of God's education, He chooses the ground rules. Well, his face was the final blow and I became frozen in silence for Lord knows how long. After some time I simply said, *Let us pray*, and the forty-five-minute workshop became a four-minute nightmare. I do not know how many kids came up to me and said, "I am sorry," and "Oh, I felt so bad." I wanted to go drown myself in a lake. The sad part about it was that not one adult talked to me and helped the issue, and yes, I was set up to fail. But the next years would bring to me a deep desire to have an audience of one, the Lord Jesus. He is my security, and if I have a gift to share, I will share. Neither the praise nor the problems of people are mine; that all belongs to Jesus. Preaching to teens is a passion and strength today. Thank you, Lord.

"For as many as are led by the Spirit of God, these are sons of God," (Rom. 8:14). The word for son in Greek is *huios* and is related to our process of hope. As I began this book, I related how important it is to know your identity in Christ. A *huios* is just that, one who is affirmed by his daddy that he is precious and valuable. That will never change. One who is converted and needing constant attention must be given the picture that they are an heir, a son. This fact may not sink in for some time. But salvation will not progress, or be effective or fruitful, if there is not a revelation that one is a *son*. There is a Greek word that describes a full-grown, or beloved son, and that word is *huiothesia*. This is well explained when John the Baptist took Jesus out of the baptism waters. The Father spoke from heaven, and said, "This is my beloved son [huiothesia], in whom I am well pleased," (Matt. 3:17). I picture a graduation ceremony where the tassel is switched, and in this case, Jesus arose from the water with a new level of sonship achieved. It seems wrong to picture Jesus the Christ as one who progressed, but He did. Do not forget also that this graduation brought Jesus through a new door, and into a new level, temptation in the wilderness. A final stage of maturity is the *pater*, which has the implication of one who skillfully molds and shapes like a potter, a fully mature son. Jesus said in the gospels, "be perfect as I am perfect." This *pater* is one who with skilled hands, because of the Father's training, can mold with their gifts and hands. Please note these five steps, *napios, paidion, teknon, huios, and pater*, and understand the progression is God's plan in His kingdom.

At nine years old, at a children's camp around a campfire, the seeds that had been planted in me about Jesus rooted my beginning of salvation, and I began my *napios* new life. I had been choosing light over darkness, and as the spirit of adoption cried through me I grabbed my brother Steve's hand, opened up the free gift of salvation, and repeated the sinner's prayer with him. (See Romans 8:15.) My full revelation of sonship was still many years of believing and receiving and confessing away, but He was still crying through me. The key, believing and confessing, have established all of my Christian foundations. Biblically, salvation means deliverance, healing, prosperity, as well as being saved from the punishment of death. Thank you, Father, for this hope of salvation that we enjoy everyday.

Salvation to born again

We do not have to get saved over and over, but we are being saved, or transformed, slowly into His image. As you believe with your heart and confess with your mouth, there will come a point where your worldly, caterpillar-like image is despised by your new heart. God's result will be a death to the old, and soon you will approach a door that many in Christianity never even open, being born again. (See Galatians 2:20.) Please note: I am not theologically trying to separate salvation and being born again, rather define for you the process.

In John 3:5, Jesus answered, "Most assuredly, I say to you, unless one is born of water and the Spirit, he cannot enter the kingdom of God." Numerous times in the New Testament you will find the phrase, enter the *kingdom of heaven*. Search the Scriptures and find that surrounding this phrase will be three major keys to entering. First, one must humble himself like a child and recognize that God is God. The second is giving up riches, or sacrificing on some level. Lastly, entering His kingdom means exchanging His wonderful kingdom keys for the old life and eternal death. Now our point at hand is, you can sit on the church pews forty years and never really hear the preacher, or maybe the preacher is not saying anything. Either way, seeing the kingdom by faith is one thing, but entering His kingdom is another story.

> Jesus answered and said to him, "Most assuredly, I say to you, unless one is born again, he cannot see the kingdom of God."
>
> —JOHN 3:3

To see or to understand, you must begin transforming from the caterpillar mentality into a butterfly. Simply put, you can enter the foyer of a great mansion and stay there forever, but that would be *boring*. Without permission or faith to *enter* all you know of this mansion is a foyer, and maybe you are not even there. You miss out on the dining room, the library, the billiard room, the kitchen, and the bedroom. How many Christians stay in the foyer of God's awesome kingdom? In John 3:5, Jesus is saying to be born of water and the Spirit. Entering that door to God's kingdom is the greatest privilege bestowed upon man. The water of the Word cleanses us unto salvation, and after that the Spirit begins to teach us how to *see* and live out this kingdom experience.

I have shared my story about the bully with Coke bottle glasses. I was most definitely saved at that time, and it seems that incident was a tremendous catalyst to help me spread my spiritual wings. It was a pivotal point at which I really could have halted the process of metamorphosis if I would have allowed unforgiveness to bloom. "But the natural man does not receive the things of the Spirit of God, for they are foolishness to him; nor can he know them, because they are spiritually discerned," (1 Cor. 2:14). Every Christian must pass through the place from the old natural ignorance to a place where we *know things spiritually.* I specifically remember the Word coming alive not long after that time. Also, I began to sit down and sing and write songs.

You must be born of water and the Spirit. (See John 3:5.) The Spirit will witness to you that you are His son as you enter. Then you must make the choice to see, at a new level, the kingdom as your nature changes in new birth. Can we cut off or quench this seeing any time in this walk *if we desire*? According to Matthew 5, to see God's kingdom you must be pure in heart. The battle that takes place for purity and spirit eyes is intense, and the key, I feel, is well explained in Revelation 12:11.

> And they overcame him by the blood of the Lamb and by the word of their testimony, and they did not love their lives to the death.
> —REVELATION 12:11

The key to being born again is your testimony. If you

were an ugly caterpillar with potential within to soar above the prairies, what would you do when that fabulous birth took place? You would shout it loud and strong. When you receive salvation, it is more personal and individual, believing and confessing. But in John 3:7 Jesus said to Nicodemus, "You must be born again." One must sense the urgency and seriousness of this miraculous gift given to man's spirit. I believe the result of being born again will be increased testimony. Paul, with great emphasis, in Romans 1:16, said, "For I am not ashamed of the gospel of Christ." My testimony is the power in salvation. When you are truly born again you will soar—enter into the heavenly places, and you will see—have a spirit of understanding. So confession begins the salvation process, and the testimony in your mouth will continue that process.

To review: conversion = darkness to light; salvation = believing and receiving; being born again = living with and sharing your testimony. Now let us dive into the awesome river of Holy Spirit baptism.

Born again to Holy Spirit baptism

I think the most momentous evening in my life was when I was throwing snowballs at cop cars (do not even think about trying this at home). We would stand behind some bushes and wait for the city police car to pass, bomb him with two or three snowballs, and run like the dickens. Naughty, naughty. Not quite as bad as Saul the Christian killer, but bad is bad. The next thing I remember is jumping over a green fence by our front porch, not knowing that walking into the living room would change my life forever.

Leading up to this moment was quite a process, as I have

explained how I lost my friend after he was poisoned by false doctrine. It would be a few years later when he took his life. My dad and mom had been searching, and had found some books and music relating to the Holy Spirit. Soon our whole family was receiving the Holy Spirit. Now I realize that my heart for unity, and crossing denominational lines, is falling on shaky grounds at this moment. I have one simple thing to say: make sure you are born again. Read Acts, Corinthians, and much of the epistles, and you will find this *exchange* with the Holy Spirit to be authentic.

As I entered the living room, a few members of my family were gathered, crying, and doing strange things. My brother Steve said, "Would you like to pray to receive the Holy Spirit?" I said, "I suppose." The Spirit seemed to say to yield up the old ways. With conviction, I broke from the inside as fears melted and His love poured over this adolescent being. I sensed the spirit of adoption and His acceptance as if I, a running teenager, were truly loved. The gentle Holy Spirit began to speak, "I want to give you more." So as my brother and family knelt and prayed with me I took a step of faith and something released within my inner being. This simple step of faith seemed to release a fire hydrant on the inside, but manifested in a meager trickle from lips that were untrained. What a cleansing flow. And yet pains and fears were evident, because by yielding to the Holy Spirit, death had to begin in the old man. The Spirit seemed to say, "You are being changed forever, you are on a walkway to holiness, and you will never be your own person again."

The author of the universe requests His presence to live and abide, and you will set captives free and minister to the broken-hearted. An incredible cistern was tapped into that day. To think of my life without the fullness of the Holy

Spirit is inconceivable. But again, the manifestation on my lips and the lifestyle is an art that I am still working on. He was sent to live in me, move through me, and increase the character of Christ through me. I could take much time in the adventures of the Holy Spirit, His gifts, His fruits, His purpose, and His personality, but my purpose here is to show you the progression.

Here is the key to Spirit baptism:

> For Christ also suffered once for sins, the just for the unjust, that He might bring us to God, being put to death in the flesh but made alive by the Spirit.
> — 1 PETER 3:18

The way to progress in God at every level, and especially full maturity, is to learn how to die. His ultimate example of death can translate into our ultimate victory. As we put to death the old deeds, the Spirit will take us to new heights. Colossians 3 says to put to death the deeds of the flesh, and its guaranteed result will be honoring the Holy Spirit. We must affirm the Holy Spirit, the promise, the comforter, and the blessed doer of the Trinity. On a personal note, I have seen folks who claim that they are baptized in the Holy Spirit, but the proof is their fruit. Remember, lordship and fruitfulness define one who is sealed by the Holy Spirit. Gifts, fruit, and calling together must be the ultimate goal, and these manifestations from the precious Holy Spirit will be as different as who you are as individuals.

Another Biblical step, according to Matthew 3:11, is the baptism of fire. This is the process of fire burning away the chaff and impurities. First Corinthians 3 explains it by listing items such as gold, silver, precious stones, wood, hay, and stubble. I know what I would like my foundations to be if I were tried by fire and it is not hay and stubble.

James says to count it all joy when you fall into temptation. But everyone knows that when this fire comes you need fireproof foundations. Do you dare to let Him baptize you with fire? When thrown in the fiery furnace, Daniel's three friends had a fire on them that exceeded the king's hot fire. In Acts 2, tongues of fire rested on the one hundred twenty, and they were baptized in the Holy Spirit and soon after were testifying.

Remember, John the Baptist said Jesus would baptize you with the Holy Spirit and fire. It is true that dying, and being broken, and being tried by fire is no one's idea of fun, but it is God's process. So our progression results from confessing and believing the water of the Word. By the work on the cross you enter this kingdom, the Spirit ignites, mobilizes, and gives you eyes of understanding. Then as one begins to die to self, they begin to submit themselves constantly to the fire of the Holy Spirit. We are all filthy and wretched, but by the Holy Spirit of fire our destiny is *pure gold*.

Again lets review the progression of hope in the kingdom and please identify where you are in this process. First is conversion, and the key: walking from a place called darkness to a place called light. Second is salvation, and the key: believing with your heart and confessing with your mouth. Third is being born again, and the key: declaring your testimony (confessing with your mouth at a new level). The final reward for those who diligently seek Him is Holy Spirit baptism, and fire baptism, and the key: a choice of your will to die to self.

HOPE HIGHLIGHTS

1. The essence of absolute hope is the ability to endure when the status quo is to give up.

2. Chosen ones who produce abundant ripened fruit are very few; these are people who nurture their hope seeds into mature faith fruits.

3. Conversion is being drawn from the Father to Jesus and walking from darkness into light.

4. In the issues and trials of my salvation I will share my gifts freely, and neither the praise, nor the problems of people, are mine—they belong to Jesus.

5. If one is born again, they have a testimony. There are three keys to the new life of entering into Christ's kingdom:
   a. Become like a child.
   b. Give up and sacrifice to some level.
   c. Exchange kingdom keys for old keys of death.

6. One baptized by the Holy Spirit is one who has learned to die to self completely. Lordship to Jesus and fruitfulness define one who is sealed by the Holy Spirit.

CHAPTER 6

The Progression of Hope—
The Potential of One Called
Follower, Disciple, Shepherd,
King, Priest, Apostle

W E HAVE DEFINED the process and progress in your walk of salvation. There is another parallel process that happened as Jesus called His disciples. This process will define the pattern that must happen as believers become ministers. A good universal vision, or goal, for Christians is that every believer would be a minister. That was a vision statement of a church I once served in. No matter what your occupation, gift, or age, the Holy Spirit wants you as His agent until Christ returns. Jesus made His calls, not in the synagogues, but at seashores, tax desks, and businesses. All chosen ones begin by considering these words from Jesus, "Follow Me."

THE GREATEST MEASURE

To follow is simple and it begins the pathway toward being mature in God. If you think of a child, and the Greek word *akoloutheo* (to follow), the following defines the beginning process of growing up:

1. To accompany
2. To go with on the roadway
3. To go the same way with

When He had called the people to Himself, with His disciples also, He said to them, "Whoever desires to come after Me, let him deny himself, and take up his cross, and follow Me."
—MARK 8:34

A story from the archives of my childhood occurred when I was seven years old at a church picnic. My friend Ricky and I were in a foot race. Now Ricky was a little older and a lot faster, but the key was that we were close friends. The race began, and not twenty feet into the race, I fell flat on my face. Our friendship was tested quickly when by sheer reflex I yelled out, *Ricky*! Promptly, he turned around, stopped, and waited until I got going again. Although he won the race, the voice of a friend outmatched his success in the fierce race. I remember the crowd laughing at my goofy cry to be saved from my distress. This is the trust that Jesus calls for. The question is who do you follow, and how much do you trust them? To accompany Him without regard of career or personal gain is quite a thought. Then to proceed on His pathway of the cross, by faith, is very powerful. Walk with me now as we reach the next level, discipleship.

And whoever does not bear his cross and come after
Me cannot be My disciple.
—LUKE 14:27

To choose discipleship is to make a calculated decision
to change the old ways and begin to believe (adhere to,
cling to, trust in, rely upon) the one you are following.
The Greek word for disciple is *mathetes*, which means:

1. To learn
2. Math, thought through with effort
3. One who follows the teaching, and the teacher

This takes following to the next level and zeros in on the
teaching and the character of the teacher. There comes a
time when you must ask the question, do you trust Jesus?
Do you really believe in this cross that is heavy and difficult to bear? Are you willing to use God's plan of submission to one more godly than you? The number one thing
in my life that has caused me to grow spiritually has been
leading those who would follow. Once I had a friend who
was very talented and had amazing potential in ministry.
We already had walked through the hardest roads, watch-
ing the Lord heal much of a very fractured childhood. At a
crucial point in his walk, dealing with relationships and the
flesh, he chose to switch his trust over to another friend.
After paying the price for years of victory it seemed that
his other friend offered a cross of a little less weight. I truly
was not offended. But no one knew him like me, and at a
pivotal point he chose to forsake our bond.

A lifetime curse was being broken from deep inside him,
and overnight our friendship, its covenant, and its protec-
tion were nonexistent. The price was incredible confusion

for my friend. He was married, and months later he came back in great agony as we attempted to pick up the pieces. The end of this story was divorce.

> If anyone comes to Me and does not hate his father and mother, wife and children, brothers and sisters, [in comparison to God] yes, and his own life also, he cannot be My disciple. And whoever does not bear his cross and come after Me cannot be My disciple.
> —LUKE 14:26–27

In the previous chapter, which parallels this chapter, we said that a testimony and dying, are keys to salvation. Being a disciple will require the same sacrifice, and we must love God.

When you follow the teaching, and the teacher, you can become a disciple. As we continue, remember hope's pathway will urge you and provoke you to be His chosen vessel. It will begin with a response to follow His call. Then, by building trust in His character, you will become a disciplined follower. Eventually, your gift will make room for you.

Disciple to a shepherd

The chance to make disciples will come in our life, but the battle for this great commission is intense. Just how many seeds do we have to plant before it sinks in to one we are training? The answer to that question may be to look in a mirror and reflect on your progress over the years. A look in my mirror brings many memories and many struggles toward a place where I was mature enough to reproduce. One memory is from my first youth pastor position, and I was learning disciplines of study, prayer, and public speaking. On one impressionable evening, a teenager humbled me with a great lesson. I was teaching ten to twelve kids on a certain topic, and, although I was enjoying myself, there was only one person taking notes. I preached really hard at that one faithful young lady. She received my *spiritual* award for the day until I approached her afterwards. I said with a little pride in my voice, "Got some notes on my message tonight, huh?" "No," she said. Then she proudly gazed at her notebook, looked up at me, and with a voice that seemed to carry halfway through the county, she said, "Tonight you spoke for twenty minutes and in that time you said the phrase 'ya know' one hundred twenty-five times." I looked at her paper, and sure enough she had one hundred twenty-five marks on it. That night I was cured of saying *ya know* during a message.

I want to help you identify where you are in your walk. How many people give up after an incident like I just described and say, "No way, I cannot handle the rejection." Motivation defines the graduation of a disciple to a shepherd. A truly gifted shepherd will not need credits or applause, but will simply and naturally be surrounded by trainees. After defining discipleship, a great way to begin painting the shepherd's picture is to compare this person with a hireling.

> But a hireling, he who is not the shepherd, one who does not own the sheep, sees the wolf coming and leaves the sheep and flees; and the wolf catches the sheep and scatters them.
>
> —JOHN 10:12

The hireling flees because he is a hireling and does not care about the sheep. Another common name for this person is pastor. Let me emphasize here that I am not referring to the leader of a church. In Romans 12, Paul is listing ministry motivations. The list includes giving, mercy, rulers, prophecy, ministers, and teachers. Please note that these motivations are different than the fivefold gifts in Ephesians 4:11–12: apostle, prophet, evangelist, pastor, and teacher.

I have three statements that I would like you to ponder. First, I believe there are many shepherds, or pastors, that never stand in pulpits at a church, and God never intended them to; they just simply shepherd their world. Second, I am also strongly of the opinion that some of the most effective fivefold ministers are ones who became seasoned in the workforce, fulfilling their motivation as mentioned above, and then after years of God's training they become effective fivefold ministers. Third, I also know many are placed in an awesome pulpit of responsibility and do not belong there at all. Man has elevated many young and talented people, and older ones, that have progressed to a place of ministry before their time. The result is the opposite of God's plan to develop a person. The biblical definition of shepherd (*poimen*) is:

1. A herder of sheep
2. Guides, cherishes, leads
3. Protects, gives life for sheep

This describes the shepherd in John 10 who is like Jesus and is our perfect example. My purpose is to convince you that you should strive to gain these qualities, no matter who you are. When belief in Christ matures in you, this will be the natural progress, and you will begin to disciple more and more. You say, 'I have no desire to be a shepherd and produce disciples?' If you plan on being a mom or dad, and if you are a Christian, you should consider this:

> Go therefore and make disciples of all the nations, baptizing them in the name of the Father and of the Son and of the Holy Spirit.
> —MATTHEW 28:19

If you feel like you are excluded from this, okay, but we must take this personally and understand the Lord's plan. Each one will answer for themselves at the final judgment. To make it clear, moms are shepherds of their flock, and so with teachers, CEOs, and coaches, among others. Although each one has a different purpose, there is a similar gift. To take the gospel of Jesus seriously, disciples must be made. Why fight God's plan?

As previously mentioned, someone who is not just saved, but born again and Spirit-led, is a person with a testimony and who makes disciples. How many Christians have reached this place? A good answer would be one who begins to guide, lead, love, protect, and give his life for Christ's sake. Those qualities demand absolute humility, servitude, sacrifice, and ultimate authority will follow. At no level is a pastor a *lord* or *dictator*, but one who gives his life and serves. When a pure shepherd's heart from the Father becomes *defiled*, control is often the result. If this is an issue, please go back in this book and define words such as *shame*, *judgment*, and *defraud*.

So a follower follows until he, with detail, has learned from his teacher and becomes a disciple. Then, as maturity takes place, many will surround you, and you will begin to function, guide, and cherish as a shepherd.

A shepherd to a king and priest

Posture is a word that comes to me when thinking about entering into the presence of royalty. The process of becoming a follower, disciple, and shepherd will literally begin to show up in your physical stature. In seventh grade, not long before the Holy Spirit came on the scene, I was pretty much driving my teachers crazy, and you could find my posture deeply slouched in my classroom desk. One junior high English teacher told my folks, "He is an angel at times and a devil at other times." At that point in my life I was searching for someone to follow and hoping to find hope. The Lord brought many instruments of different kinds to help me with my sullen posture. What a contrast to compare confusion, indecision, and childhood with a king standing arrayed with endless authority. That is what began to take place a few years later when I received the Holy Spirit. It is not hard to identify those who walk as a king and priest, because their posture is upright, but with great humility and excellence. The humility part is not man's requirement, but a paramount God requirement. Picture again the caterpillar that has the qualities to be an airborne king.

Once again, the process is so important and you must believe, even as a caterpillar, that He, a king, is in you! In the Old Testament there were three kinds of people who heard God's voice. They were prophets, priests, and kings. The normal Joe simply was not expected to be personal with the God of Abraham, Isaac, and Jacob. If you study closely the kings were not God's choice, but man's choice. Over hundreds of years a majority of the kings did not serve God and many were wicked. What a mess! Apparently, God's plan until Jesus came was for the prophets to give the spiritual direction and see God's path for the nation.

The priests were to be the go-between, and carry out the Mosaic commandments regarding sacrifice. But man wanted a king to rule and even though it was second best, the Lord granted it. This reminds me of the church today. The Lord has set up a government with Christ as the only king, and we as servants of various kinds are to be the eyes, ears, hands, and feet of His kingdom on earth. Instead we have set up our little kingdoms and organizations, some of which are enormous, and, to cut to the chase, man gets honored more than God. I am very concerned about the *state* of the church today and it is related to issues of control, power struggles, and building our own kingdoms instead of unity.

> That they all may be one, as You, Father, are in Me, and I in You; that they also may be one in Us, that the world may believe that You sent Me.
> —JOHN 17:21

In the context of this book we build kingdoms in the name of faith and when it is all said and done a great percentage of pastors end up crashing and burning. Christ's name gets a bad rap. My friends, that is not faith. In the name of love, we hastily throw up buildings, open the doors to our church, get the people into a program, or into a protestant, catholic, or charismatic ritual, then demand giving for the debt we have incurred and call that love. My friends, that is not love. I am totally convinced that faith and love are acknowledging our frailty, bowing before the king consistently, believing, enduring, being innocent of evil, washing feet, and serving until Christ is formed in us.

85

His fruit of love and faith will then be manifest. Again, the greatest time spent in God will not be about faith and love, but hope. The faith and love of Christ will be manifest through enduring hope. It is like eating a hard peach, or sweet corn premature; you cannot enjoy an unripened or undeveloped fruit. So it is with faith and love. But a great piece of fruit or corn: my, my, my, so it is with love matured through hope.

> And from Jesus Christ, the faithful witness, the first-born from the dead, and the ruler over the kings of the earth. To Him who loved us and washed us from our sins in His own blood, and has made us kings and priests to His God and Father, to Him be glory and dominion forever and ever. Amen.
> —REVELATION 1:5–6

Jesus rules over everything and has all power because of His blood, hallelujah! To see yourself in this high call from Revelation is to see your life engulfed in the Spirit of God. The kingdom pathway, even as Jesus became a king, was seeing, hearing, and doing. If you clearly interpret the Bible, true authority comes through humility. There is a grace when you are a child, but as crimson colors of progress appear on your battle cloths, then comes the real test. You either become an agent with God in His grace or a *king me* to honor self. Every person's goal should be to walk in this royal authority and with great humility. The Bible clearly states that God will reject the prideful, and if one would bow in a posture of meekness, God will cause him to soar like a kite.

Humility

K   Knowing your place, and knowing God's place.

I   Intimacy resulting in the fear of the Lord.

T   True realization of need.

E   Experiencing godly sorrow.

There are three words that I feel describe kings and priests: chosen, excellence, and wisdom. The first one requires a seasoned character, and attitude.

To be chosen

> You did not choose Me, but I chose you and appointed you that you should go and bear fruit, and that your fruit should remain, that whatever you ask the Father in My name He may give you.
>
> —JOHN 15:16

If God chooses you, you will not need to publicize it, you will simply walk in it and bear fruit. One who walks in this capacity and authority is one that has not taken shortcuts, but has shuffled through and defined the good and acceptable and stands in God's perfect will. This person does not need to be called *king* anymore than one *needs to be called* pastor, teacher, or prophet. Anyone who needs that recognition definitely has something missing. On the other hand, people who see them as such will honor someone that walks as a chosen one.

> Coming to Him as to a living stone, rejected indeed by men, but chosen by God and precious.
>
> —1 PETER 2:4

The Greatest Measure

> He is Lord of lords and King of kings; and those
> who are with Him are called, chosen, and faithful.
> —Revelation 17:14

Make a marquee of those three words, and when it is
all finished, faithful will be the greatest compliment ever
given to you. Remember, the makeup of faithful is *hope-ful*. What are we doing here? We are defining the hopeful
process of one called. A king is one who rules a king-dom. This might be a corporation, or a business, or your
household, or, for a young person, your bedroom. These
places that define the location of your dominion will be
defined by truth or lies, good or evil, pure or defiled, just
or unjust. You are the king of your domain and it is your
choice to make the Holy Spirit a part of your *temple* or
not. A priest is one who performs the sacred rites of God.
In context to kings, priests, and humility, we must share
the following story:

> And they withstood King Uzziah, and said to him,
> "It is not for you, Uzziah, to burn incense to the
> Lord, but for the priests, the sons of Aaron, who
> are consecrated to burn incense. Get out of the
> sanctuary, for you have trespassed! You shall have
> no honor from the Lord God." Then Uzziah
> became furious; and he had a censer in his hand
> to burn incense. And while he was angry with the
> priests, leprosy broke out on his forehead, before
> the priests in the house of the Lord, beside the
> incense altar. And Azariah the chief priest and all
> the priests looked at him, and there, on his fore-head, he was leprous; so they thrust him out of that
> place. Indeed he also hurried to get out, because the

LORD had struck him. King Uzziah was a leper until
the day of his death. He dwelt in an isolated house,
because he was a leper; for he was cut off from the
house of the LORD. Then Jotham his son was over
the king's house, judging the people of the land.
—2 CHRONICLES 26:18–21

This story is self-explanatory; do not tamper with God's
plan! Leprosy is a manifestation of a powerful type of
pride. It has a root of independence, of *you* being on the
throne, and it slowly begins to eat away your flesh unto
death. First, a king and priest is one that is chosen; next,
he must have a spirit of excellence. One of the greatest
historical figures of excellence was Daniel. This young
man went through the fire of testing and, at the end, made
decisions in a kingly posture in the presence of a king.
An excellent spirit, knowledge, understanding, interpret-
ing dreams, solving riddles, and explaining enigmas were
found in Daniel. (See Daniel 5:12.) Dying and sacrifice
were the earmark of Daniel's exemplary life. Of all of the
great prophets, kings, and priests in the Bible, few had
Daniel's record of *no recorded blunders.*

But we have this treasure in earthen vessels, that the
excellence of the power may be of God and not of us.
—2 CORINTHIANS 4:7

The word *excellence* means *to throw beyond, excess, superi-
ority.* Picture numerous doors that are labeled "follower,"
"disciple," "shepherd," "king," and "priest." In time, the
Spirit of God plays the graduation music, and you excel
through the next door. As we have mentioned before, you
can *see* the mansion or, through obedience to the Spirit, you

89

can enter the fullness of His kingdom. Each door brings new warfare and new blessings. Each success spreads hope inside you that emanates one truth: in Christ nothing is impossible. Not necessarily material riches or position, but excellence is a true mark of a king and priest.

Next, a king and priest display understanding and wisdom. "There is a man in your kingdom in whom is the Spirit of the holy God. And in the days of your father, light and understanding and wisdom" (Dan. 5:11). The ultimate jewel in Proverbs is wisdom, "and in all your getting, get understanding" (Prov. 4:7). We have already said that understanding is the hope of God's counsel, and wisdom is the ripened fruit of knowledge. A prayer to memorize is:

> That the God of our Lord Jesus Christ, the Father of glory, may give to you the spirit of wisdom and revelation in the knowledge of Him, the eyes of your understanding being enlightened; that you may know what is the hope of His calling, what are the riches of the glory of His inheritance in the saints, and what is the exceeding greatness of His power toward us who believe, according to the working of His mighty power.
>
> —EPHESIANS 1:17–19

As we conclude this ministry process of hope, see yourself as an ultimate light reflector with a posture on your knees, entering the most holy place, and excelling with kingly wisdom in every task of life. Whether you are a burger flipper at Burger King or a multimillionaire, the posture of a king and the poise of a priest unto God is your choice. According to Jesus, it is actually much

90

more difficult for the millionaire than the burger flipper. I would like to paraphrase a story from *The Final Quest* by Rick Joyner.[1] The Lord took Rick on a journey through a part of heaven, and he was observing some of the greatest kings in mighty places in heaven. He observed a king sitting there with angels serving him that he noticed was a tramp who lived in a cardboard box on earth.

> Angelo had received Jesus through a tract that drifted his way. Though he was deaf, he sold pop cans to buy gospel tracts. He set his little cardboard box up at night as a mighty house of worship. He thanked the Lord more for an apple than most of us do over a great feast. The Lord helped him lead a dying alcoholic to Christ before he went home, as thousands in heaven and all the angels were waiting for him. He was honored as maybe few in history ever were because of what he did with what little he had.

I love this story, and it is convicting because we all must do something with what He has given us. Kingship is not about finances, status, and inheritance, but the inheritance through Christ into His glorious kingdom of hope. A final ministry stage is being an apostle. After a long journey from following Jesus to being a disciple, to a shepherd, king, and priest, we find a few rare *potter* servants who walk consistently in signs and wonders, establishing churches, and with consistency, this person can touch each fivefold ministry. Each other area that we have covered includes areas in which most expectant Christians with faith expectancy can attain over time. I believe there are apostles today who are called by God but with very, very high standards.

> Therefore, holy brethren, partakers of the heavenly
> calling, consider the Apostle and High Priest of our
> confession, Christ Jesus.
> —HEBREWS 3:1

In Ephesians 4:11–12, the fivefold ministry gifts are included, and in the church, the apostle is the most undefined and often very misunderstood. If one continues in a posture of humility he may become the ultimate sacrificial warrior for God, a potter, an apostle. This figurative thumb of the hand will touch the pastor, evangelist, prophet, teacher, and I believe function in each one. This person will have regional, and often national, exposure and has intense responsibility. I again see three definitions that define the apostle:

1. One who has consistent visible spiritual encounter with the resurrected Christ
2. One who plants churches, can function in, and touch all ministry gifts
3. One whose ministry includes signs, wonders, and miracles

"Truly the signs of an apostle were accomplished among you with all perseverance, in signs and wonders and mighty deeds," (2 Cor. 12:12). Many self-proclaimed apostles can be identified because they are missing the ingredients. Please do not try to complicate this process, just pursue it and walk in who you are in Christ. Those who function effectively as an apostle will have walked in consistent ministry for two to three decades and probably more. Defining each process should help us appreciate the ones called to it or spur you on as you continue your journey. Remember, you have Jesus as the high priest of your confession, and, as a king, you will rule in life by the power of His blood.

The hope of one blessed and not cursed

One last gem for you: one who walks in their complete anointing will walk in blessing. Choose one of the two: blessing or cursing. You can read Deuteronomy 28 and find all the blessings and the curses. But as I was studying one day I stumbled across an interesting difference between the two. In a nutshell, curses consist of poverty, sickness, and death. Blessing is a combination of three things: poverty, brokenness, and death. There is one element that is different and, of course, in Christ the other words have a different meaning. To identify the curse would be to gaze at this mighty world. I will not prolong the poverty, sickness, and death aspects, but let us touch on the highlights.

> I do not pray that You should take them out of the world, but that You should keep them from the evil one. They are not of the world, just as I am not of the world.
>
> —John 17:15–16

This world is cursed with poverty of heart that ironically results in deceitfulness of riches and a life chasing after the almighty dollar. People are in a journey to cover up their shame and fear, and they end up in a sick state of spirit, soul, and body. The final result for one *not in Christ* is the punishment of death.

To be blessed, you must enter the Matthew 5:3 poverty and in that humility you will see God's kingdom. Next, let the Father break your heart and let your weakness become His strength.

> The sacrifices of God are a broken spirit, a broken and a contrite heart—these, O God, You will not despise.
>
> —PSALM 51:17

As with the lady that came to Jesus with a vial of precious ointment, our brokenness is of the highest value to our Lord. Lastly, as we have talked about, death to self is the ultimate key. Dying to self will be Christianity's resurrection blessing to your life. If you are sick physically, or have a sick heart of pride, you need Christ's completed work on the cross. He was wounded for your healing, and broken so you can be broken and contrite, the only pathway to being a king and priest unto our God. (See Isaiah 53:3–5.)

To review the ministry progression of hope: the heart of ministry begins as a follower, then a disciple. This can progress to one who leads disciples and followers, a shepherd. An ultimate place of humility and servanthood could bring one to a calling of king, priest, or even a New Testament leader or apostle.

HOPE HIGHLIGHTS

1. To follow is to accompany, to go with on the roadway, or to go the same way with.

2. A disciple takes following to the next level, and zeros in on the teaching and the character of the teacher.

3. A shepherd guides, leads, protects, cherishes, and gives life for those under him. Motivation defines this stage. This person does not need credits and applause, but will naturally be surrounded by people.

4. A king, priest, and prophet unto God will have a posture of humility, excellence, wisdom, and often will walk from one called to one chosen.

5. A curse consists of poverty, sickness, and death. Three things will define one blessed:
   a. Poverty, meekness of spirit;
   b. Brokenness, a broken and contrite heart; and
   c. death to self.

CHAPTER 7

Hope Defined

HOPE IS HUMBLING, beholding, yielding, submitting, and waiting on the Spirit of God. Be not conformed to this world, but be transformed by the renewing of your hope that you might prove what is the good, acceptable, and perfect will of God. Hope is the transforming agent of the mind if its base is God's Word. Hope is the conditioning and dying to self, the strategy and discovery of the opponent. Hope is one thousand hours of practiced shots, so that when there are five seconds left in the last quarter of the game, by faith you make the shot. Hope is the battle, faith is the victory. Hope is the hearing of faith; hope is the seeing in doing. Hope is in, hope is on, hope is through, and hope defines the process. Hope is the expectation, the drive, the pistons, and the dividing light from darkness. Hope is the clapping, the dancing, the shouting, the kneeling, and the expressing of your heart. Faith and love transform from those expressions that have occurred. Hope

96

is not wishful thinking. Hope is insight, persistence, and stubborn bullheadedness. Hope is confident expectation based on solid certainty. Hope is the happy anticipation of good. Hope is the makeup of faith, the preface to faith, and the extension of faith. Hope is confident in grace's future accomplishment. Hope is the verb side of grace; grace acts out, and breathes, and gives hope. Hope is crying, praying, waiting, and travailing until your Isaac has been birthed from a miracle called grace.

> Who, contrary to hope, in hope believed, so that he became the father of many nations, according to what was spoken, "So shall your descendants be."
> —ROMANS 4:18

Hope is that even in utter tragedy and stupidity, God can give a *door*. Hope is expectation, yearning for, and in anticipation eagerly waiting. Hope is something for which one waits, to bind together by twisting. Hope is smelling the bread of life. Hope is thirsting for the water of life. Hope is hungering for the meat and maturity of life. Hope is touching the hem of Jesus' garment; faith is receiving virtue from Him. Hope is what we are saved in. (See Romans 8:24.) Hope is our anchor, but we are secured to the faithful and loving rock, Jesus Christ.

Hope is embracing the Father God, and *knowing* His embrace. Hope is defining the curse, and receiving Christ's redemption. Hope is reflecting on Him with thanksgiving. Hope is sacrificing to Him through praise. Hope is birthing God's very presence through knowing Him in worship. Hope is the planting of God's seed. Hope is the dying of the seed. Hope is the resurrecting of the seed. Hope is weathering the storms after you have popped through the soil. Hope is waiting for your purpose (fruit) to be made manifest and enduring its tests. Hope is waiting for ripened fruit until it has manifested. Faith and love is that fruit in you that identifies a true disciple. Hope is the tasting of the Holy Spirit, love is embracing Him. Hope is expecting the promise, water, submersion, and fire of the Holy Spirit. Hope is the desire to be sealed by the Holy Spirit. Hope is developing Spirit fruit, the proof of that seal. Hope is patient, kind, and the process of never being jealous, boastful, or proud. Hope is bearing all things, enduring all things. Hope is believing, adhering to, clinging to, trusting in, and relying upon all things. Hope is holding on to God's promise. Love is the 1 Corinthians 13 product of that incredibly long process. Hope is saying and not doubting in your heart. Hope is following until you become a disciple. Hope is enduring until you are a shepherd. Hope is dying to self until you walk as a king and a priest unto your God. Hope is the wooing by the Father God, and being converted. Hope believes (adheres to, clings to, trusts in, relies upon) unto salvation. Hope is seeing you as a caterpillar and being born again with an incorruptible seed. Hope is being submerged and catapulted into the excellent and precious promises of the Holy Spirit. *Hope in Christ will be the greatest measure of your life!*

The door of hope

> I will give her her vineyards from there, and the Valley of Achor as a door of hope; she shall sing there, as in the days of her youth, as in the day when she came up from the land of Egypt.
>
> —HOSEA 2:15

As we continue to define this wonderful hope, let us reflect on a very hopeless moment in Israel's history when, in Joshua 7, Achan sinned against God and Israel. His single act for a chunk of gold condemned the flow and victory in battle for all of Israel. It all took place in this Valley of Achor mentioned in our verse above, which means trouble. As a result of his sin, Achan and his family all were stoned to death, and a historical marker was set up to remind all their descendants of his stupidity.

Hosea 2 tells a story that defines God's potter's wheel of hope in the midst of ruin. In Jeremiah 18, hope is defined as a ruined vessel of clay, but is made a totally new thing by the hand of the potter. Even out of utter tragedy and stupidity, our God will give a *door of hope* where singing and joy can return. The Valley of Achor, a historical curse and place of trouble, now according to Hosea is a door of hope and a place of celebration.

The rope of hope

Let us go back a few chapters in Joshua and talk about the harlot Rahab as she helps Israel in an act of kindness, hiding Joshua and Caleb. Of the thousands in Jericho, God chose this harlot to be delivered and honored by becoming a part of the lineage of Jesus, as she was King David's great, great grandmother. The salvation of her entire household was contingent on a scarlet cord.

> Unless, when we come into the land, you bind this line of *scarlet cord* in the window through which you let us down, and unless you bring your father, your mother, your brothers, and all your father's household to your own home.
> —JOSHUA 2:18

THE GREATEST MEASURE

The scarlet cord is a symbol of history's greatest hope, redemption. Rahab is the symbol of the least in the kingdom becoming the favored, and the blessed. Let us specifically define the word *hope* in this passage. The word for cord in this Joshua passage is *tiqvah*, or literally, a cord of hope that brings redemption. Tiqvah: *expectation, yearned for, and anticipated eagerly, something for which one waits.* Definitions of words often evolve and become contemporary in order to enhance the meaning. But *tiqvah* originally was translated *line, or cord.* The deliverance for this harlot's entire family, out of a doomed city, came directly through a scarlet cord of hope. The word *stronghold* (which Rahab provided) in the Old Testament has a direct connotation to a refuge of hope. The words hold fast, stand fast, and steadfast in the New Testament also speak of something being bound together, holding on, and waiting in hope. Most know of the eagle passage, Isaiah 40:31.

The word *wait* in Hebrew literally means *to bind together by twisting.* Now you tell me how high you would soar if you would do that daily with the Creator of the universe? Let me earmark my favorite "faith, hope, and love" scripture:

> Remembering without ceasing your work of faith, labor of love, and patience of hope in our Lord Jesus Christ in the sight of our God and Father.
> —1 THESSALONIANS 1:3

This scripture so well describes the eternal trinity of faith, hope, and love. In the context of defining hope, notice the hope words that preface these three eternal legends, *work*, *labor*, and *patience*. You see, love and faith are the greatest, but as defined in this verse, even they will be surrounded by hope in order to come to fruition. This New Testament word *hope* is the Greek word *elpis* and is defined, "not wishful thinking, but confident expectation based on solid certainty, the extension of faith, and confidence in grace's future accomplishment."[1] This helps us understand how we are saved through hope. The Lord's redemptive cord will always provide and define a door of hope in the midst of trouble.

The prisoner of hope

Let us conclude by defining hope in apostle Paul fashion, as a prisoner of God. Truly, the most difficult assignment on earth is to live as a servant of Christ. But there is also no reward on earth that can compare. Do you understand that our destiny is to be slaves to righteousness, bound by His love, and persecuted for our stand in Christ? It is incredible that Paul wrote most of the epistles from prison. And I struggle to concentrate from my leather recliner. We complain when we have to fast for a few days, or pray for an hour, or deal with a friend who needs counsel. A prisoner is one who is being held against their will inside a stronghold of some kind. Like it or not, this Christianity thing is usually a decision that goes against your will and your plans. Instead of pride and independent living, life in Christ is servanthood, humility, and death to self. Zechariah has a powerful thought on this:

> As for you also, because of the blood of your covenant,
> I will set your prisoners free from the waterless pit.

> Return to the stronghold, you prisoners of hope. Even
> today I declare that I will restore double to you.
> —ZECHARIAH 9:11–12

A dry, horrible pit pretty well describes the spirit of this age. Now when I say this I do not mean on the surface, this generation has become masters of facades, cosmetics, and carnivals. I love Psalm 40:1–3 (author's paraphrase):

> I waited (hoped) patiently for the Lord, and He heard my cry. He brought me out of a horrible pit, and set my feet on a hard firm path and steadied me as I went along. He put a new song in me that others might see and believe, and put their hope in the Lord.

The prison switched from despair to a house of worship. Zechariah 9 mentions two more things. First, the blood covenant is the only basis for true imprisonment to God. If you want light or a clear conscience, it must be by the blood of Jesus. (See 1 John 1:7; Hebrews 9:14.) Lastly, the Lord will restore double the blessing that you once had living in your fake world. We must choose His blood covenant, head for the stronghold of God, and get behind those prison bars of surrender, the ultimate place of hope.

HOPE HIGHLIGHTS

1. Consider the following descriptions of hope. Hope is beholding, yielding, waiting, transforming, battling, clapping, dancing, praying,

expecting, smelling, thirsting, touching, embracing, exchanging, defining, reflecting, sacrificing, birthing, planting, desiring, developing, enduring, saying, seeing, and knowing. Hope is confident expectation based on solid certainty.

2. Remember that the makeup of faith is hope. The greatest measure of your life in Christ will be walking through the process of hope to bring you to wonderful pinnacles of faith and love.

CHAPTER 8

The Mountain of Hope

THIS CHAPTER REPRESENTS the cornerstone of why I wrote this book. I am truly convinced that hope is a consistent, missing vital element in the body of Christ. The mountain of hope and its journey will reveal the learning, grueling, tantalizing parts of life in Christ that define reality. Reality is not revival to revival, church service to church service, and from blessing to blessing. Reality and truth are unveiled and found in John 8:31–32: "If you abide in My word, you are My disciples indeed. And you shall know the truth, and the truth shall make you free." The reality of righteousness is revealed from faith to faith. (See Romans 1:17.)

The *to* between faith to faith is the issue at hand. The makeup and the endurance test of faith is hope. Always remember that without hope, you do not have faith; hope is the makeup of faith. I believe this means that faith is the first measure, and hope is the greatest measure, until by faith you act again on what the greatest measure, hope, produced. (See Romans 12:3.) The mountain of hope is the process that will give you great faith.

The mountain of hope

> As His divine power has given to us all things that pertain to life and godliness, through the knowledge of Him who called us by glory and virtue, by which have been given to us exceedingly great and precious promises, that through these you may be partakers of the divine nature, having escaped the corruption that is in the world through lust. But also for this very reason, giving all diligence, add to your faith virtue, to virtue knowledge, to knowledge self-control, to self-control perseverance, to perseverance godliness, to godliness brotherly kindness, and to brotherly kindness love. For if these things are yours and abound, you will be neither barren nor unfruitful in the knowledge of our Lord Jesus Christ. For he who lacks these things is shortsighted, even to blindness, and has forgotten that he was cleansed from his old sins. Therefore, brethren, be even more diligent to make your call and election sure, for if you do these things you will never stumble.
>
> —2 PETER 1:3–10

Let us begin by touching on verses eight and nine. If these things are in you, you will neither be barren or unfruitful in the knowledge of Jesus. As we unfold the mountain of verses four through eight, understand that they are the keys to a fruitful life. One who neglects and refuses these things will be shortsighted and blind. The last verse of 1 Corinthians 13 unveils the structure of this mountain. Three eternal things will remain: faith, hope, and love, and the greatest is love. There are eight significant, eternal things that make up this mountain. Faith is the starting point, the entrance key with grace to salvation, and the pleasing hallmark that explains almighty God Himself. Six tough elements contain the heart of this journey, the reason for this book. In Christ, hope is life's greatest measure. These six things are virtue, knowledge, self control, perseverance, godliness, and brotherly kindness. The final reward will be one powerful pinnacle, the bond of perfection, and that by which all of the law is fulfilled in one word, love. For a church that has an epidemic of barrenness, shortsightedness, and blindness, I believe the climb I am about to define is huge for the end time church.

The foundation—the work of faith

The starting place, the first level of humility as we charge upward is faith. If you have just been saved, or if saved for fifty years, each new door or starting point will be opened by faith.

> Looking unto Jesus, the author and finisher of our faith, who for the joy that was set before Him endured the cross, despising the shame, and has sat down at the right hand of the throne of God.
> —HEBREWS 12:2

Jesus is our ultimate example and the author of our faith. Hope is the *and* between author and finisher of our faith. Hope is not the greatest, but the greatest measure. Faith is not even the greatest, love is. When Jesus said of the centurion, "great is your faith," do you see that the compassion and power of love was the greatness that truly

106

brought the healing? Faith and hope defined the necessary vehicle.

Each believer, according to Romans 12:3, is given a measure of faith. There are no favorites in God's book. Receive Him, and with Him comes a measure of faith. The sinner has something like faith that attracts him to the spirit of adoption. Frankly, I do not fully understand how the Father draws the sinner, but I know he does. "Add to your faith" (2 Pet. 1:5) is the first charge as this mountain begins. You cannot please Him without faith, and the first seed He plants within us is faith. Faith and faithful basically define God's desire and requirement for our life. What will be the words you hear from the Master when you graduate to heaven? *Well done thou good and faithful servant?* Faith is a muscle that must increase in order for us to increase in Him. Weak faith must be highlighted, defined, and exposed. Can you argue that hope is the main ingredient of faith, and weak faith tells us that the ingredients are weak? The current, immediate strength or portion of the faith that you possess is the substance of everything that has passed the invisible but tangible test of hope. (See Hebrews 11:1.)

What is the difference between the first place winner of a marathon, who by faith and confidence receives the prize, and the person in last place who falls over the finish line in hopes of never running again? The answer is the work of faith. Faith without works is dead. Actually, a type of faith without works can exist, but it is something fake, or manmade, not God-made. The God kind of faith always has the work of hope as its base, or makeup. We live in an age of a self-confident, self-reliant, fast food faith. Never forget that it is Jesus who is the author and finisher of our faith. Any foundation other than His blood, His hope, and His seed will never please God. 1 Corinthians 3:10–13 calls these good foundations gold, silver, and precious stones, and the proving is a test of fire. People are fruitless, lazy, unmolded, and fleshy because they do not have the foundation of work (hope), and faith without works (hope), is dead. According to 1 Corinthians 3, some people have foundations of wood, hay, and stubble that fiery trials will consume.

To deify faith itself is an error in the body of Christ that I have seen for many years, and the balance is hope. According to the famous Mark 11:22–23 passage, you cannot move the proverbial mountain into the sea just by faith; it must be *the faith of God, or the God kind of faith.* You must (hope) believe, adhere to, cling to, trust in, and rely upon God, and say, and not doubt in your heart, then the mountain will move. Do you see how believing is hope? God's faith has a powerful, enduring, verbal, expecting foundation to it. Sorry, but believing is work, not a fast-food approach. It is not by works that you get anything from God; it is by grace, through faith. Just after I was engaged to my wonderful bride, the Lord really stretched my faith and challenged me. We were quite tight in the area of money and anticipating a wedding in the future. Cathy's car was in very bad shape, but mine was in quite good shape. We were in a service in which a lady was in need of a car, and the Lord prompted me strongly to give her my car. I thought, *Oh you mean give her Cathy's car. Well you will have to talk to Cathy about that.* He said, *No, you give your red car to this lady.* Early on He was teaching me that He deserves our best. By God's grace, I passed this tough test, and I ran to her and handed her the keys to my car immediately before I changed my mind. Long story short, we have not had a car payment for about half of our marriage.

So as we begin this journey up the mountain of hope, faith and its righteous seed from Jesus is what we get to add to. What a foundation!

> Therefore, leaving the discussion of the elementary principles of Christ, let us go on to perfection, not laying again the foundation of repentance from dead works.
>
> —Hebrews 6:1

God's issue is progression toward maturity (perfection). We must leave the baby stages of repentance and faith as we keep them secure in our foundation. By faith, you will stand at the base of this mountain, and you must choose to charge forward and upward. No one will make you. Then you must accept, define, and perfect the ingredient that make up strong hope. Roll your sleeves up, get on your hiking boots, and come on.

The yoke of virtue and knowledge—2 Peter 1:5

Please consider a yoke in this context to represent two things tied together. If you drew a picture, the Mountain of Hope would look something like the following: the bottom plateau before you begin your climb as I have explained would be faith; halfway up the first side of the mountain would be the beginning of hope, virtue, and knowledge. The long picturesque walk on the top would define patience and endurance. Down the other side would be a period called hopeful godliness and brotherly kindness, and on the final plateau, valley, and the final reward to this eternal mountain would be love. Without trying to spoil a punch line later, when you complete this particular mountain you must continue on, and the Lord will ask you to start all over again with a bigger mountain of hope. This eternal process never quits.

Let us begin by defining virtue as separation of light from darkness. The very first, elementary, and basic principle after having faith in God is dividing light from darkness. This in essence is the first grace the Lord bestows upon his new children. What were symbols that showed growth in Christ for you when you were converted? Most would have an answer such as, "I quit drinking, smoking, partying, and bad language." Define how you excelled in that conviction process, and you will define virtue. Virtue is defining the difference between good and bad, darkness and light, and choosing light.

Did you have some years in Christ which seemed much more ruled by your flesh than Christ? What a battle when the Lord is training you to listen, and your stubborn will bucks against Him. I was not a terrible sinner; I just had a few years in which I could not obey. Alcohol and drugs, no problem; I never touched the stuff. My problem was religious pride, which Jesus publicly condemned.

What is the reality and judgment of the woman caught in adultery and myself who has never had a beer, standing next to each other? In Jesus' eyes, I was actually a worse case because I had the goods inside to prevent my sin. My pride was deep, my rebellion was pathetic, but I did have a desire to serve my Savior. However, it took several learning experiences to learn my lesson.

Once, when I was in grade school, I leaned over to

sneak a peak at a cheat sheet in one of those older desks with the space for books under the seat. The problem was there were holes on both sides underneath. When I saw the teacher coming I pushed the book and it flew into the isle and almost hit her in the feet. I could never get away with my sin, but I did desire to change. Go ahead and laugh, I deserve it, and I got a big goose egg on that paper. You have your own stories, but sin is sin and Christ's kingdom is in us to remove that old nature. Virtue is translated excellence, in some versions of the Bible.

> If there is any virtue [excellence] and if there is anything praiseworthy—meditate on these things.
> —PHILIPPIANS 4:8, AUTHOR'S PARAPHRASE

Daniel is one of the Bible's best examples of excellence. The first five chapters of Daniel show his pattern of *separating himself* from even the king's pleasures unto a place of excellence.

> There is a man in your kingdom in whom is the Spirit of the Holy God…Inasmuch as an *excellent spirit*, knowledge, understanding, interpreting dreams, solving riddles, and explaining enigmas were found in this Daniel…
> —DANIEL 5:11–12, AUTHOR'S PARAPHRASE

Daniel has one of the most unblemished records of any Old Testament hero. He understood separation. From the first, when he was handpicked out of Babylon, Daniel chose God's way to live and eat instead of the king's way. Daniel divided right and wrong, and ultimately set the example as one who would serve his God no matter what anyone thought. The final test was life or death in the lion's den, where he saw blessed deliverance. What made Daniel understand and divide right and wrong? It seemed stupid to eat salad and water instead of pork and the king's succulent food and wine when his very life was at stake. But his excellence, his power to see, and the ability to follow through what he saw was amazing. You can eventually see God's purpose in this virtue as King Nebuchadnezzer was changed.

In addition, Shadrach, Meshach, and Abednego received a miracle anointing from his virtuous wisdom. Saul is our new covenant example of being divinely sanctified (set apart) unto God. After being knocked off his horse and struck blind, he had to separate himself from his religious piety unto a new kingdom of light. Saul, who became Paul, has to be the greatest story of one hopeless in sin and finishing his race as possibly the most influential vessel of light in history, besides Jesus.

> For you were once darkness, but now you are light
> in the Lord. Walk as children of light.
> —EPHESIANS 5:8

I love the story in Luke 8:43–48 about the woman with a chronic blood disorder. A seed of hope and desire that was in her made her break all the rules. She had no business in public, and no business receiving healing apart from the stubborn faith that made her press through the crowd. When she reached for and touched His garment, power and virtue went out from Jesus and light was instantly separated from darkness. The result in this case was healing. The result in Philippians 4:8 of this same virtue is a renewed mind. So as we head up this mountain of hope, the first yoke and plateau that we must embrace is virtue, yoked with knowledge. Virtue is the process of dividing darkness from light, and knowledge is simply you dedicating yourself to the light.

> For it is the God who commanded light to shine out of darkness, who has shone in our hearts to give the light of the knowledge of the glory of God in the face of Jesus Christ.
> —2 CORINTHIANS 4:6

This is the Lord's example, a light switch is turned on in the darkness, and knowledge becomes the result. Knowledge includes facts and things you know. It is a seed that begins its journey on a pathway to understanding, and finally, wisdom.

> For this reason we also, since the day we heard it, do not cease to pray for you, and to ask that you may be filled with the knowledge of His will in all wisdom and spiritual understanding; that you may walk worthy of the Lord, fully pleasing Him, being fruitful in every good work and increasing in the knowledge of God.
> —COLOSSIANS 1:9–10

Do you see the progression toward wisdom? If you walk in the light and walk pleasing to Him, you will increase in knowledge. In adversity, you will soon birth the hope of God's counsel—understanding. I shared earlier that most of the body of Christ never increase to strong disciples, but stay followers. Most never really take wings and fly as one born again, but stay, settling for the elementary stages of salvation. Most never push through a place where they separate light from darkness and choose holiness. Most never see the significance of knowing God and dedicating themselves to the light. Most never see the picturesque, colorful, challenging mountaintop called self control and perseverance.

Remember 2 Timothy 2:15, "Be diligent to present yourself approved to God, a worker who does not need to be ashamed, rightly dividing the word of truth." Excellence and diligence are a choice of the will that few attain. Notice that even truth needs to be divided. False doctrine and ignorance come when people only get half-truth on a matter and have not rightly divided that truth. The written Word of God is not a theory, but factual information about our awesome God. Rhema is the Word divided, and spoken personally from God's lips to your heart, and your circumstance.

God's spoken word is what will bring virtue and knowledge into your life. After faith and repentance, you must divide, light from darkness (virtue) and then gain knowledge. Proverbs 1:7 says that "the fear of the Lord is the beginning [or for most, a part] of knowledge." Folks who find themselves backsliding back down to baby faith and repentance must learn the fear of the Lord. The posture of humility, and a deep, awesome respect for almighty God, will always be the pathway to the rhema of God.

Self-control yoked with perseverance—2 Peter 1:6

You might say self-control and perseverance should not be on the top of the mountain, but on the hard upward stretch. Those words just seem like hard work. I believe that the hopeful process of virtue and knowledge define most of the entire grueling climb up the mountain. Of course you learn self-control and patience in that process, but there seem to be tests that graduate you to the next level. Past virtue and knowledge, you have now graduated from a *grueling tedious mountain climb*, only to find a *jungle*.

Self-control defines a place in your Christian walk where you conquer foolish habits. This proverbial flesh jungle will train you to be slow to anger and one of a *sound mind*. Psychology may be man's way, but God's way is this process that begins defining your sin nature and ends with the Holy Spirit's fruit of self-control.

Romans 12:1–2 pleads for transformation, and a renewed mind will prove His good, acceptable, or perfect will. This self-control, sound mind, or temper control is a fruit of the Holy Spirit in Galatians 5:22–23. The contents of a fruit is discovered when it is squeezed or opened. Picture yourself finally passing the test of virtue and knowledge, and you are relaxing in your recliner contemplating this door called *self-control/perseveranc*e. You finally take the courageous step through the door only to see a jungle of cares, deceit, and lusts ready to choke you in any moment of weakness. In this boot camp to maturity you must face disciplines such as fasting, praying, solitude, meditation, and simplicity. These flesh killers help define this marathon stretch on top of hope's mountain. Who cares how flat the terrain is? Just thinking of the word *fast* is enough to make you backslide very quickly, unless you are READY!

No matter where you are on this mountain, do not forget Hebrews 12:2, "Looking unto Jesus, the author and finisher of our faith, who for the joy that was set before Him endured the cross." A very transparent story of mine clearly defined entering this door of self-control/perseverance. I was sixteen or seventeen years old and it was time for my written driver's exam. I was taking some divine exams in virtue and knowledge and approaching my test into self-control. Comprehension in school, and in the Spirit, was my biggest problem. The point was really driven home when I had studied for this driver's exam and planned on getting it over with and getting into my wheels. I took the test, and bombed it. Okay, we will get it done the next time. The next time came around and I got one more wrong than was required. In my own way I hit the books and, to my dismay, embarrassingly bombed it a third time. No, I am not telling you that I am stupid; I am telling you that I could not shortcut this one and a very hard life lesson was staring me in the face. The fourth time, the sweet port of entry lady felt sorry for me and helped me correct a few problems in order for me to pass. My climb up Mount Virtue-Knowledge was a hard one. But to this day I can tell you of many principles that sank deep into my understanding through this hard climb. From that day, after passing that test, and for the next four years, my heart was set to gain knowledge and virtue. I began memorizing Scripture and defining my sin of laziness and deceit. I entered into a very unvirtuous relationship, and after heartache and dividing dark from light, God graciously saved me from immorality. Those lessons still are rewarding today.

Entering into self-control/perseverance began when I entered Bible college. When I went to the port of entry in Oklahoma to take my written driver's test, everything was different and as I took that test with confidence, I was not the same. I passed with only one wrong the first time on that test, and I was on my way to more doors of discipline.

A key element: authority

> Now when Jesus had entered Capernaum, a centurion came to Him, pleading with Him, saying, "Lord, my servant is lying at home paralyzed, dreadfully tormented." And Jesus said to him, "I will come and heal him." The centurion answered and said, "Lord, I am not worthy that You should come under my roof. But only speak a word, and my servant will be healed. For I also am a man under authority, having soldiers under me. And I say to this one, 'Go,' and he goes; and to another, 'Come,' and he comes; and to my servant, 'Do this,' and he does it." When Jesus heard it, He marveled, and said to those who followed, "Assuredly, I say to you, I have not found such great faith, not even in Israel!"
> —MATTHEW 8:5–10

What was it that impressed Jesus so about this centurion? If you compare other miracles such as healing the blind, demoniacs, and prostitutes, Jesus' powerful virtue touched them and they were whole. Many times Jesus asked them what they desired, and they asked Him to fulfill their need. Understanding authority is a cornerstone to God's kingdom. This is the place on the mountain that many never reach, and God-control and persistence will be the key.

> And Jesus came and spoke to them, saying, "All authority has been given to Me in heaven and on earth."
> —MATTHEW 28:18

Not some of the authority, but all of it belongs to Jesus. Then in the Great Commission Jesus gave us authority to cast out devils, speak in tongues, and lay hands on the sick. (See Mark 16:15.) Understanding authority has everything to do with patience and nurturing the elements of hope unto great faith. A frequently occurring theme in this book is: *this posture did not happen overnight; great faith does not happen overnight.* For this centurion, expectation and hope were so great that nothing mattered; time, distance, or circumstances. All that mattered was that if Jesus spoke the word, it would be done. Something formed that understanding in him, and that something was an understanding of authority. The process of going and coming that came from a simple word defined this boldness and success.

Self-control is giving the Spirit of God control and submitting to his authority. Perseverance defined is that regardless of the circumstances, you *will not give up*, and you will have God's character through trials. In Luke 18:1, Jesus said to always pray and not faint and give up. He explained again in Luke 11:5–9 that prayer is one knocking and asking until, through persistence, he receives. It is safe to say that this leg of the journey is where your prayer life will be seasoned, or prove barren. You see, persistence, insight, and stubborn bullheadedness absolutely, positively define hope. Remember Romans 1:17; the revealing (or revelation) of righteousness is from faith to faith. This strength and support beam again defines the "to" of faith. The God kind of hope just does not give up. And do not forget that in Christ, righteousness is what is revealed from faith to faith. A result of your grueling climb will be right standing with God in Christ.

A good example would be one of our righteous seeds,

Timothy, our son. We have talked about the birthing process and all of the elements that bring great hope. Our first son is one who was revealed and birthed through long perseverance. We nearly wore out a cassette tape called *Peace* as an anticipated few hours of labor turned into a marathon of forty hours. The revealing of our glorious first offspring gave us quite a lesson in endurance. My Cathy, who is a beautiful example of endurance, through many of her contractions pictured herself climbing a mountain (very fitting) and asked me to help her over the mountain. It was a test for her stamina, strength, and grit, and the doctor was very impressed. I am sure she represents a very small percentile of women who labored that long without delivering the baby through surgery. Anyway, the reward, and the glory on the face of our Timothy, were well worth the titanic endurance test. Cathy and I can boast of having a master's degree in patience regarding things such as buying and selling houses, furniture, dining room tables, bicycles, cars, vans, vacation packages, living room portraits, and clothes. Go ahead and laugh; I know you have been there. We could give you a personal marathon story of each of the above items. I am so thankful that I understand that the Lord gives us these trials to build us, not torment us. Can anyone say *AMEN*?

The following was found tacked on the wall belonging to an African pastor:

> I am part of the "Fellowship of the Unashamed." The die has been cast. I have stepped over the line. The decision has been made. I am a disciple of Jesus Christ. I won't look back, let up, slow down, back away, or be still. My past is redeemed, my present makes sense, and my future is secure. I am finished and done with

low living, sight walking, small planning, smooth knees, colorless dreams, chintzy giving, and dwarfed goals.

I no longer need pre-eminence, prosperity, position, promotions, plaudits, or popularity. I now live by presence, lean by faith, love by patience, lift by prayer, and labor by power. My pace is set, my gait is fast, my goal is Heaven, my road is narrow, my way is rough, my companions few, my Guide reliable, my mission clear. I cannot be bought, compromised, deterred, lured away, turned back, diluted, or delayed.

I will not flinch in the face of sacrifice, hesitate in the presence of adversity, negotiate at the table of the enemy, ponder at the pool of popularity, or meander in the maze of mediocrity.

I am a disciple of Jesus Christ. I must go until heaven returns, give until I drop, preach until all know, and work until He comes. And when He comes to get His own, He will have no problem recognizing me. My colors will be clear.

But we all, with unveiled face, beholding as in a mirror the glory of the Lord, are being transformed into the same image from glory to glory, just as by the Spirit of the Lord.

—2 CORINTHIANS 3:18

The self-control of beholding Him and understanding His character is the *to* in glory to glory. Do you have the audacity to hang onto a passion to shine with His glory as our African pastor above? What does the word *transformation* mean to you? Not revivals and church services, but walking day-to-day, faith-to-faith, and glory-to-glory.

The key to 2 Corinthians 3:18 is that the Spirit of the Lord's purpose for us is glory, but the *process* of obtaining it is beholding Him. Hope is not His glory in and on you; that glory is the final product. Hope is the yielding, beholding, confessing, and *waiting* for that process to happen. One who stands in awe of someone is one who understands their authority.

The heartbeat of hope: tribulation

Have you ever felt your physical heartbeat after strenuous exercise or before public speaking? A simple example of proving that your heart is there inside your chest is to put pressure on it. Pressure is a necessary God ingredient in the process of life to determine the invisible spiritual condition of one's life. Please note that trials are not always demonic attacks; trials can be God's significant learning experiences for us. Since the fall, adversaries have legal access to us, as weeds gained legal access onto the soil. The natural penalty of sin has brought stress on all creation. But our God is always with us to conquer those foes.

A childhood memory came to mind as I was honored to sing with my brother and a friend at a city holiday gathering. The song was the classic "This Land Is Your Land." However, I was to sing a solo on a verse that started with, *I roamed and rambled.* Memorizing the verse was not a problem; I just could not get the phrase, *as I went walking* out of my head, which was the first verse. When I woke up that morning, I said the phrase *I roamed and rambled, I roamed and rambled* probably five hundred times, right up to the time when we were to sing, as my heart was pumping through my chest. If only I could begin the song with the words *I roamed and rambled.* The lovely rendition was going well, until we got to my solo, and I opened my mouth and sang, *As I went walking*. I immediately realized I had goofed and I froze in my spot. My alert friend, Dave Laposky, with his guitar, quickly bailed me out as we sang the first verse again. This type of pressure has happened many times to me through the years.

> And not only that, but we also glory in tribulations, knowing that tribulation produces perseverance; and perseverance, character; and character, hope.
> —ROMANS 5:3–4

Perseverance has quite a prestigious place as a preface to character and, of course, hope. Although not a fun subject, tribulation and suffering challenge the heart. As you surge forward on this mountaintop, you will find out this endurance test will shake and test your foundation. Proven character will be the test of this pivotal part of life. Character is what you do when no one is looking. Character is what you approve with your mind.

> My brethren, count it all joy when you fall into various trials, knowing that the testing of your faith produces patience. But let patience have its perfect work, that you may be perfect and complete, lacking nothing....Blessed is the man who endures temptation; for when he has been approved, he will receive the crown of life which the Lord has promised to those who love Him.
> —JAMES 1:2–4, 12

The maturing that happens, if you allow patience to complete, is God's plan. The result will be a wonderful crown of life, which is rewarded, according to James, for those who love God.

A final note on this leg of the climb up Mount Hope is that tribulation and perseverance will be an excellent preface to persecution. Persecution is a realm that few ever allow themselves to reach in their faith. The Beatitudes in Matthew 5 give good insight into this progression. First, Jesus says *purity equals seeing* (seeing light and dark) and then blessing for those who mourn. Obviously one who is mourning is one who has gone through something traumatic. So one sees through purity, and there is blessing for those who mourn. A little later He says, *blessed are those who are persecuted for righteousness' sake, for theirs is the kingdom.*

Persecution will happen only if you are emanating God's glory and truly sold out for God. Second Timothy 3:12 says, "Yes, and all who desire to live godly in Christ Jesus will suffer persecution." This commitment will bring you down Mount Hope from this wilderness of wait to a place where the desolate and hurting are waiting for a word of hope.

Before we enter the next exciting door, these questions from previous chapters might help. Are you ready to pass from born again to Holy Spirit baptism? Are you ready to move from a disciple/shepherd mentality to a place where you are ruling as a king and a priest unto your God? If so, you are probably ready to pass through the wilderness of wait.

Godliness yoked with brotherly kindness—2 Peter 1:7

Let us review our mountain so far. God begins our

journey with a seed of *faith*, which is at the base of Mount Hope. Mount Hope's six principles, made up of three yokes, begin by separating light from darkness, virtue, and dedicating ourselves to the light, knowledge. We graduate through a door called self-control and perseverance. Hallelujah, we have passed the test of the fleshly desert, and, in a nutshell, we are on our way to effective ministry.

In the context of this book, *effective* is something that must be defined and lived out daily. This leg visually is a downhill cruise, but as we strive toward love's doorway, we find ourselves with more responsibility than any other level. This is where your character and preparation bring you to 1 Corinthians 12–14 and Galatians 5, manifesting gifts and fruits of the Holy Spirit. Do not forget Mount Hope's goal in 1 Peter 1:8,10. If you have these things and abound, you will neither be barren or unfruitful. And if you *do* these things *you will never stumble*! That is incredible! How many times does the Word declare these kinds of statements regarding your maturity? I am glad you asked! There are five "never" promises in the New Testament, and they are all good ones. The other four will be very familiar to you. In the gospel of John, Jesus declared that if you know him, you would never be hungry, thirsty, or you would never die.

And in the classic 1 Corinthians 13, "Love never fails." I have heard it said that God is the only one who can say never, and my strong point is that these hope statements must be pretty special if they are agents of never stumbling. We will highlight later the fact that love never fails. Paul mentioned godliness twelve times to Timothy.

124

> But you, O man of God, flee these things and pursue righteousness, godliness, faith, love, patience, and gentleness.
>
> —1 TIMOTHY 6:11

Now this verse clearly affirms all my Mount Hope ideas. Flee darkness, pursue, gain knowledge of righteousness, and compare the remainder; they match perfectly with our process. We have spoken earlier of posture that is typical of a king. Godliness/brotherly kindness speaks of posture from the inside/outside. God gives responsibility to ones that can handle it. God will resist someone very talented with a posture of pride. The opposite is true of a godly person; humility is written all over their posture.

> Having a form of godliness but denying its power. And from such people turn away!
>
> —2 TIMOTHY 3:5

The greatest insult to Jesus is hypocrisy. Study His moments of outrage in the gospels. Hypocrisy is pretty on the outside, ugly on the inside. It is quite evident that a characteristic of godliness is the presence of Christ's power in a person's life. The words *control, potential,* and *supernatural* define power in the New Testament. Are you ready to give the Holy Spirit everything so that you can be graced with His power? That is a great question, because today's ministers have used *control, and potential,* and *supernatural* for their own gain; and without the Holy Spirit, that is very scary. I could use many examples and superlatives here, but I will just quote one short verse of scripture. "I never knew you," (Matt. 7:23). That is the ultimate hopeless curse on life: to be a minister of the gospel and have Jesus announce those words to you when the journey is done. You had great gifts, you prophesied, but you never knew Jesus! If you were reaching the sunset of your life, what would your autobiography look like? The power of the gospel is that the prophetic Old Testament concealed becomes the New Testament revealed. Our ability to prophecy is similar, and in some ways advanced, compared to the Old Testament prophets. We have the Holy Spirit living right inside of us. The words we speak are prophetic and powerful, and it does not matter if you believe that or not. You say, *I just do not like to talk about spiritual things a lot.* Out of the abundance of your heart, your mouth will speak. As you reach places of responsibility in your life, are you afraid to uncover the real you, or is your life, inside and out, a reflection of the Word of God? I will not linger here, but instead, give you a poem I wrote which can wrap your hope story in a nutshell.

MY AUTOBIOGRAPHY

> Today as I walk in God's prophetic Word
> There is an endless source of truth to be heard.
> The Spirit's invitation to claim your holy promise
> Gone are the days, and ways of doubting Thomas.
> Incorruptible seed He has planted deep with-in,
> It is origin Christ's blood, now I am free from sin.
> A fountain, a river believing with my heart,
> Each morning, noon, and night, I have to do my
>   part.
> Possessing my prophetic promise, a choice of my
>   will,
> Speaking words with my mouth persistently until,

126

The candle He lit will turn into a sweet burning
light.
The sacrifice of my lips, my ears, and of my sight,
A burning torch of peace, joy, understanding divine,
The Spirit of wisdom, revelation, and riches all are
mine.
Spirit hope producing faith, foundations strong in me,
As I speak the truth in love and write my autobiog-
raphy.
Written each day with heaven's ink, by almighty
God,
As I fight and possess with diligence my milk and
honey sod.
With eagle eyes in the air my holy hands will raise,
To heaven above two wings of prophetic prayer and
praise.
Now it begins, I open my mouth, a life river flow-
ing free,
From your Word, Lord, I begin to write my autobi-
ography.

But you shall receive Power *when the Holy Spirit* has
come upon you.

—Acts 1:8

Being saved and confessing Christ is common. But
going further, prophesying and yielding to the Holy
Spirit constantly is peculiar and defines *the few, the humble, and the godly.* "As His divine power has given to us
all things that pertain to life and godliness, through the
knowledge of Him who called us by glory and virtue," (2
Pet. 1:3). Have you ever met a true gardener, who from
the depths of their being displays tender loving care and
knows how to produce the best and most beautiful life?

That is a good example of this leg of the journey. It begins with selfless kindness, tender loving care, and a character that only comes from endurance. One who is godly is one who multiplies the fruit of their labor. This person knows when to prepare, plant, pull weeds, and when to reap. Defining this downhill slope is important, because it will be difficult to manufacture kindness and morals when in the ghetto of the poor and needy. It will be difficult to cover up fleshly strongholds when Satan sets up a trap of lust and pride. If you have cheated the process, you will cave in at the door of one chosen. If you are cruising on a pathway of performance instead of the power of childlikeness in the Holy Spirit, you will soon roll into the swamp of despair!

This despair will be a bitter pill and will hinder your return to the process of eternal Mount Hope. If at virtue/knowledge on this journey you fail or are disqualified, simply grab your mentor's hand, repent, and try again. But the judgment, and penalty, will be much greater to one proven godly. You should have several followers that are under your care by this time, and disqualification for whatever reason will be devastating to many. We have had too many examples of this failure in the body of Christ over the past years. Please walk through the process of hope and qualify yourself through a posture of humility to bring brotherly kindness and godliness into your life.

The bond of maturity/love

> Therefore, as the elect of God, holy and beloved, put on *tender mercies*, *kindness*, *humility*, *meekness*, *longsuffering*; bearing with one another, and forgiving one

another, if anyone has a complaint against another;
even as Christ forgave you, so you also must do. But
above all these things *put on love, which is the bond of
perfection.*
—COLOSSIANS 3:12–14, EMPHASIS ADDED

Before we begin, notice another confirming verse filled
with hope words. Love has a wonderful foundation, and,
when built properly, it is perfection. But it must be well-
constructed on faith and hope. Remember, faith works
(hopes) by love. Love stands alone; it is the greatest, the
ultimate goal, that which fills all the commandments in
one word. And love was Jesus, God personified in His
perfect Son. If we look at our mountain of hope and
the progress we have made so far, all of the yokes, principles, and faith itself are working toward a crescendo, an
increase, a buildup, and a climax called love. Each step of
hope past the beginning faith screams for more and for
completion. Hope is the greatest measure, but hope is
painfully incomplete in itself.

Now, if after reading this book, the painful part seems
negative to you, then you have missed a huge part of
the process. If you cannot see and admit that being a
disciple is very difficult, and even painful, then I do not
have much hope that you can complete this mountain
in a godly manner. A tremendous athlete or executive is
simply sold out to the fact that they will endure endless
hours of agony to reach their goal. My love for my wife
is incredibly strong, as strong as any force that I personally know on this earth. But we have fought for that love
spiritually, financially, socially, mentally, and physically.
Any time we have reached a new level in our *exchange*

and relationship, it was probably after a 10 p.m. to 3 a.m. heavy discussion, fighting for our love. If you love something or someone, you will fight and sacrifice for that love.

In closing this thought, divorce in marriage and divorce spiritually with the resurrected Christ comes through a spineless, gutless, defrauding attitude that does not know how to fight for what truly is virtuous. Some have said, *we were divorced because of irreconcilable differences.* Someone else might say that Jesus or the pastor offended them for some reason, and they have not fellowshiped in six months. Hold on; I do have grace, and so does Jesus, if there are grounds for divorce. But the overwhelming point here is that the state of the church, and the posture of the home, is not exchange and intimacy and love. It is give up when the waves start to ripple.

Let us draw a quick picture. Jesus is sleeping on the bottom of the boat, the wind and storm intensifies, and the disciples do not know what to do. They awaken Jesus. He calms the sea with three words and then rebukes them. Why? Because even though there is danger and fear present, we are at a point in our relationship that fear and doubt should not be an option. If we do not have the sense to teach a teenager not to fool around with his girl-friend, at sixteen, then we should not be upset when they are in the divorce courts at twenty-two. This topic just angers me, and really is at the core of this love principle. You cannot cheat your way through the exchange and mountain climbing of this faith and hope stuff, and make it through the storms with a *mature outcome*. Remember, fruitfulness and maturity define the ultimate goal here.

Hope is digging down and fighting and enduring

no matter what! Faith is the positive climax of that fight, the substance, and the calm sea. Love is the light turned out at 3 a.m. after a nice long passionate kiss with a calm sea. Hopeless is turning that light out countless times in anger until finally there is no light whatsoever in your exchange, and each storm speaks of hopelessness, and in Jesus words, "little faith" (Matt. 8:26). Do you have the guts to fight for love? Do you see how, if you have fought and won each battle previously, the trials ahead become so much easier?

Hope that is unfulfilled is like a seed gone bad, or an unhatched egg, or a dream that was never fulfilled. Hope that is seen is not hope, but faith is the substance. Hope that is seen is not hope, but love is seen; it has premium, fulfilled qualities, and impeccable character:

> Love suffers long and is kind; love does not envy; love does not parade itself, is not puffed up; does not behave rudely, does not seek its own, is not provoked, thinks no evil; does not rejoice in iniquity, but rejoices in the truth; bears all things, believes all things, hopes all things, endures all things. Love never fails.
> —1 CORINTHIANS 13:4–8

There is that *never* promise that we mentioned before. True love is so foreign to our society. Let us use another practical picture. Can you imagine acres and acres of seven-foot majestic corn? Can you see the fields of golden grain blowing in the summer breeze? Sure you can, but my ploy is the unseen, unsung heroes including the soil, sun, moisture, hidden seeds, nourishment, and the lonely ninety degree nights when you can hear corn crackling up through the ground. Those underdogs produced the incredible harvest, and without them, you would have a barren field. We have already identified that those unseen things are very grueling, difficult, and make up our hope mountain. Anytime you see that maturity, finish line, and overwhelming fruit-filled achievement, you have reached the atmosphere of love. Without a defined hopeful process and a faithful substance to define its form, this love will not happen. As mentioned before, this form is gold, silver, and precious stones. These qualities are tested by hope-fire, and its end is more purity, and more worth, more love, and more power.

> Therefore, leaving the discussion of the elementary principles of Christ, let us go on to perfection, not laying again the foundation of repentance from dead works and of faith toward God.
> —HEBREWS 6:1

We are talking about going forward to the perfection of love that is built with a sure foundation, but most folks want to inherit a majestic skyscraper. Inherit a skyscraper, and you would not even know what to do with it. The Holy Spirit speaks to your heart and says, *I will give you the materials of hope to build your future, and then at the end, if you will be faithful with what you have, you and the master builder will make a skyscraper.* What we inherit is redemption, forgiveness, and mercy through the tragedy of the cross, but seasoned love is a process. Included in those drops of Jesus' blood are the qualities that make up our hope mountain. Consider a field of flowing grain, consider a powerful saint of God, or a coveted fruitful marriage full of Christ. Each mentioned went through the process to eventually define a portrait of love.

So where do we go from here? Do we now stand in a place perfect and ready to walk on water and save the masses? Well, I would like to jump back onto our mountain and walk you through what is happening. First of all, the time period in which one completes this mountain is very uncertain. Progress is integral to success, but each has a different grace or gift to handle hope's task. I believe if you have studied this chapter you can see that this powerful process climaxes as a pinnacle of love. The beginning, the dividing, the receiving, the enduring, the molding of character, and posture toward maturity is the clear pathway to God's kingdom. Even Jesus went through that process! So here we stand in a place of contentment, with clarity and vision bursting from our countenance.

Let me draw a final, crucial picture for your consideration. The final stretch of Mount Hope is full of responsibility, discipline, and developing a level of love for this stage in your life. At this point there is something in each of us that is ready for the gold medal or a graduation ceremony. *Come on, throw me a party, or print my accomplishment in the newsletter.* Our prize is the high calling of Jesus, but our selfish eyes create a cosmic door with a secret penthouse, pool, and a permanent vacation. Error and false doctrine are born at a selfish place where people are satisfied. Their posture is turned away from the cross, and *me and my accomplishments* become the goal.

It is amazing what one can justify through the Scriptures when there are wrong motives, to the point of drinking poisoned Kool-Aid and manipulating and killing your own sheep. In over twenty years of ministry, I have never seen that extreme, but I know what its perverted seed looks like and have defined its makeup. Yes, I have had to kill those *pride seeds* in me on a number of occasions. The truth, however, turns your posture toward the cross and the enduring joy that is in Jesus, our example. Let me share the following scripture at this point in our mountain.

> In labors more abundant, in stripes above measure, in prisons more frequently, in deaths often. From the Jews five times I received forty stripes minus one. Three times I was beaten with rods; once I was stoned; three times I was shipwrecked; a night and a day I have been in the deep; in journeys often, in perils of waters, in perils of robbers, in perils of my own countrymen, in perils of the Gentiles, in perils in the city, in perils in the wilderness, in perils in the sea, in perils among false brethren; in weariness and toil, in sleeplessness often, in hunger and thirst, in fastings often, in cold and nakedness—If I must boast, I will boast in the things which concern my infirmity.
> —2 CORINTHIANS 11:23–27, 30

To hope for the penthouse with the pool and all its pleasures is so far from the heart of God. Now to say that I am against the prosperity message would not be true, because I live debt free, like a king. True hope is living the life described in that verse and leaving a legacy. For the apostle Paul this included his writings and uncompromising spirit. Hope's end will fulfill the purposes of God and bring you to Ephesians 4:13, "Till we all come to the unity of the faith and of the knowledge of the Son of God, to a perfect man, to the measure of the stature of the fullness of Christ." If someone has a pool, we will come on our day off, and if I get one, we will have a party; but do not mix pleasure with the incredible purpose of God, to labor in love for Christ.

So let us turn toward the next door. No do not look back or even dwell on your accomplishments. Friend, what is through that next door, after one level of maturity in Christ, is a mountain; Mount Hope. However, this mountain is about twice the size of the one that you just journeyed. It contains the same eternal qualities, but a new level of understanding in them. This process *can* go on until you are done with life on earth. If you want *great faith* and the *perfection of love*, you must continue this process. You know what I love about this? I love the fact that if you have been walking Mount Hope for two months or fifty years, there will always be a common denominator. Those that have walked it longer will have some great advice for the beginners. When life is through, heaven will reward faithful people and those who look like Jesus. Yes, some rewards will come on the earth, but the vision is to be like Jesus, and the result is good fruit. Your greatest measure and time spent will become your greatest attribute. Your effort will produce honor or dishonor, and either love or something that counterfeits love.

HOPE HIGHLIGHTS

1. Any foundation other than the blood of Jesus, and hope, and His righteous seed will never please God. The God kind of faith has a powerful, enduring, verbal, expectant foundation to it.

2. Virtue is the separation of light from darkness. Knowledge is you dedicating yourself to the light.

3. Most never see the significance of knowing Jesus and dedicating themselves to the light. Most never see the picturesque, colorful, challenging mountain jungle called self-control and perseverance.

4. Psychology is one of man's ways, but God's first way is defining your sin nature and, through faith in Christ, conquering it. This God process is called self-control.

5. The word *power* is defined control, potential, and dynamite. The characteristic of one godly is when Christ's power is evident in their life.

6. Without a defined hopeful process and a faithful substance to define its form, love will never mature in you.

7. Error, false doctrine, and being lukewarm are born at a place where people are satisfied. Their posture is turned away from the cross, and me and my accomplishments become the goal.

CHAPTER 9

It Is All About Grace

B IBLICAL WAITING IS the opposite of this world's arrogant haste. Romans 12:7 (KJV), admonishes us to "wait on ministry," but Romans 12:3 crowns grace as the key to this waiting, "For I say, through the grace given to me, to everyone who is among you not to think of himself more highly than he ought to think, but to think soberly, as God has dealt to each one a measure of faith." The posture of this verse sets the tone for the wait and the spirit of the powerful Romans 12. The makeup of faith is hope, and the measure dealt to you is essentially hope not yet developed. The point here is that the measure, which I feel is hope, will never turn faith if grace does not neutralize arrogance and pride. Let me quickly neutralize any thoughts you might be having that I am speaking against faith. I did not say that it was not faith, but I said that the measure at the beginning is hope, such as the grains of wheat in the bin that will in time be a wheat field. The long journey of each grain of wheat will need grace and hope to finish its course. Just go over that a few times. It is not as complicated as you might think. It is all about grace! I can hear you say, "Wow, that last chapter was the climax, and love should end our journey!" Simply put, salvation begins, and ends, with the grace of our Lord Jesus through faith.

Since being saved at nine years old, I have walked Mount Hope probably three or four times and I have found that in turmoil, God's grace was the scarlet rope that rescued me and the Father's strong arms that carried me. At twenty years old, this humble preacher's kid had two gifts: I loved people and I could sing. The following things I have picked up in the past twenty-two years while mountain climbing: prayer, while at a lumber yard after high school; experience in Rhema Bible Training School; janitor; burger flipper; husband; dad; youth pastor; district and regional youth director; youth camp worship with guitar; camp director; speaker at camps; associate pastor; piano player; worship leader of dozens, hundreds, and a few times almost a thousand; intercessor; counselor; children's pastor; tenures in Florida, Wyoming, South Dakota, Minnesota, and Michigan; mission trips to Mexico, Africa, Jamaica, Canada, and India; preaching to crowds of up to five thousand; evangelist in many U.S. states, with many saved, delivered, and healed. Believe me, I am not trying to brag or give you my resumé. I am simply drawing a picture of someone that began with very little and has been rewarded with more. Frankly, that is not that much at all compared to some, but for each thing He is added, I must remain responsible in the grace of God. Incidentally, I am in an incredible wilderness of wait as I write this book, and there are several questions regarding my life purpose. In context, the grace of God has provided the multiplication, and it will be only that grace that will fulfill my purpose in life. Without the hope of grace, life would be hopeless. Again, I have just clearly defined hope. Hope is being totally insignificant, like a caterpillar, and, through a grueling climb and death to self, finally grace multiplies, and destiny becomes airborne. A caterpillar reality should be trained heavily in ministry boot camp. I personally have chosen not to be just another blundering statistic of indiscretion, impatience, and pride. But it is only by His grace that I will one day be airborne into my full purpose.

Two sides of grace

The heart of this concluding chapter is to focus on the hope of hope, grace, and its characteristics, coupled with obedience. I see two descriptive wings of grace: hope and mercy. I know you cannot put parameters on Him or His grace, but I would like to describe two sides. Grace, whether its work is to forgive and pardon or to enlighten with knowledge, to declare true judgments, to strengthen in endurance, or give you ministry gifts with love, is absolutely free and without measure (notice Mount Hope). History saw hundreds of prophets, priests, and kings, and hundreds of years of *the law* wailing for a new time period. Then Jesus, who was full of grace and truth, came on the scene. (See John 1:12.) The Word became flesh, the law (for some) became grace, those in darkness had a hope of light, and salvation was born.

Many years ago I had a friend who was struggling in his marriage, and I did my best to counsel he and his wife. After dealing with the issues of these two born again believers, I remember him coming to me some time later. He said, "I got it, I got it." He went on to explain about the revelation that he felt he received about grace. I had shared with him my favorite definition of grace, *the divine influence upon the heart.* The light bulb came on and he declared, *I must receive and give my wife grace.* He had a spark of hope that pointed him to the cross and its purpose to set him free from the inside out. He set his heart to speak *grace* to this mountain in his marriage. It was one of those cases where I almost fell over, because he and his wife were very stubborn, and grace was certainly what they needed. This story does not have a good ending. The Mark 4 *good word* was not planted into a soil that could produce. As excited as he was about his revelation, he was not willing to build the foundation of wait, sacrifice, and dying to self. This was many years ago, but I clearly remember that those two were divorced within a year of his great revelation. Their foundation of independence, cares, and deceit was stronger than their desire to have the divine influence upon the heart.

If you would reflect back in this book, I have at least three stories of friends such as in the above story, and each story turned out very negative. I would have loved to have faith for them, but again, that is not how His kingdom works. Everyone has motivation of some kind, and friends like these truly give me a motivation to work on my marriage constantly and give grace. I will focus on the good stories.

Let us hike down the home stretch of this book by amplifying the meaning of grace. First of all, grace, or truth, cannot have meaning without Christ's work on the cross. Secondly, obedience is our ticket to grace's full benefit. The cross of Christ is the source, and salvation's two-word key is grace and faith.

> But God, who is rich in mercy, because of His great love with which He loved us, even when we were dead in trespasses, made us alive together with Christ (by grace you have been saved) that in the ages to come He might show the exceeding riches of His grace in His kindness toward us in Christ Jesus. For by grace you have been saved through faith, and that not of yourselves; it is the gift of God.
> —EPHESIANS 2:4–5, 7–8

We have already defined that faith is the beginning booster and power seed that begins our hope journey. I believe clearly that grace is the heart, influence, and the catalyst to the enduring journey of true hope, because it always points to the cross. There is a worldly hope that is empty and basically wishful thinking. But hope that is tied with grace and the cross is the reason for this book. Hope is the enduring process, the kindness and expectancy borne from amazing grace. Worshiping Christ will always birth hope, and grace defines the spirit of each ingredient in Mount Hope that we have highlighted.

Philippians 2 describes the birth of hope and grace that led to obedience, which led to death on the cross. To *obey* is the Greek word *hupakauo* and has the following meaning: "hear and listen attentively, obey, respond, a posture of attentiveness."[1] *Everything submitted in obedience* is another fantastic synonym of hope. Hope is hearing and responding attentively, with absolute confidence, which brings submission. Grace is only through Jesus and the price paid on the cross. No other god or sacrifice will ever be sufficient. Grace's very nature drips with mercy and an expectation that Christ's blood is more than enough.

Is it evident to you that transparency is a principle that I am absolutely sold out to? Before I speak, or sing, or enter an ordinary day, my posture toward God is that I am filthy, wretched, and no better than the worst sinner. Please hear me! Grace's ploy is that everyone, rich or poor, good or bad, scummy or kingly, has the same wretched curse passed on from Adam. But you do not have to live that way. If something from your past haunts you so that your exchange and holy living is hindered by it, you are insulting grace. Jesus takes our past, if we offer it to Him, and highlights grace's power to abolish it. We must receive that grace and walk in hope's obedience.

It was a very big weekend in my life. I had been promoted to directing a youth event that would see almost nine hundred kids and leaders in attendance. With eight months of preparation, six years of being a worship leader, and a big part in this event, I was excited. This would be my last year of directing this event, and this weekend would prove to be a cornerstone in my integrity in ministry and marriage for years to come. Though very vulnerable and transparent, I must share these stories to show you the hope of true freedom.

The day started when my departure plane needed a new windshield. Long story short, instead of arriving at 1:00 p.m., I arrived at 8:30 p.m. I was tired and frustrated, but I knew enough to understand that the enemy would do anything to mess up God's plans. I was alone and I have since learned that no television whatsoever is the wisest thing when you are alone. My grace at this time was to disarm all bad pay movies. I finished that task and called my lovely wife who was unable to make this trip. I was gearing my heart toward a powerful, life-changing weekend. I took a shower and sat down in the second room of this suite to watch something on ESPN, only to find one, two, and three channels of absolute filth available. I did a great thing again and instantly got angry, turned off the TV, and dialed the front desk. However, the devil was working hard, and the uncharacteristically snippy lady at the front desk was a real case. She said, "Well sir, it is not possible that those channels are on your TV." I argued with this lady for quite some time, with no progress. Finally, I gave up. Now the stupidity of hanging up and giving up ended in a great battle that highlighted my deep lack of character at that time.

Like Joseph with Pharaoh's wife I was trying to run, but the devil had one too many character tests. I later turned the television back on long enough to defile myself, before I almost vomited with conviction. I did get things right with the Lord and handled the front desk that night. But the next day, when I saw together fourteen people of my leadership and the worship team, including my brother, his wife, and nephew, would prove the test of obedience that still sticks today and actually gives me the freedom to share in this book. It was an incredible prayer time, with a great anointing to carry us into the weekend. But just before we were done, the Holy Spirit said, *Share what happened last night.* I said, *I do not think so; do not you see my brother over there?* I argued with Him before He said, *Look at your shirt.* I made a funny face and glanced at my theme T-shirt for the weekend to find the phrase *The*

Truth Will Set You Free. Before I chickened out, I began to bare my heart, and, oh my, that was the hardest thing I have done in a long time.

Now I have never had a problem with porn, and I love my wife more than you could know, but this step of obedience broke something way deep in a place that I would call youthful lusts. I was forgiven the night before, but grace broke something loose deep inside as I stepped out in obedience. My obedience was further tested as I arrived home in four to five days, and, with great significance, shared everything with Cathy. Again you say, *Yikes, that is too honest for me.* And in your denial and hypocrisy, you will not have freedom in unexposed areas. I have for a long time believed in the *extreme theory* in context to lusts and sins in my life (in this case, spiritual fornication). That theory drove me to magnify my sin that night, and grace helped me to expose the devil. Now when one enters into physical fornication, there is a greater consequence. The reason I will contest that adultery will never enter my marriage is because I cut off its ability constantly through transparency and a renewed mind in God's Word. Am I still capable of it? Absolutely, and to believe otherwise is stupidity, but I do not live there anymore.

As we open up the two sides of the wonderful grace of God, look at the following verse:

> Let us therefore come boldly to the throne of grace, that we may obtain mercy and find grace to help [hope] in time of need.
>
> —HEBREWS 4:16

We come, or anticipate, or *hope*, boldly into the grace of God's presence, which brings us to a receiving of mercy, which gives us hope because we are very needy.

GRACE

Mercy	Hope
Undeserved kindness	**Divine Influence of the Heart**
Authority—loving judgments (Ps. 19:9)	**Submission**—Jesus' Obedience (Phil. 2)
Meekness—state of inward power	**Self-Control**—soul rights under control
Love—mercy before acted upon	**Joy**—inward comeback when love is fulfilled
Gentleness—love's touch	**Self-control**—hope's patient posture
Peace—the inside referee	**Kindness**—hands and feet to a hopeless world

The two sides of grace include mercy and hope. Can you see how the all-inclusive spirit of grace is a river made available to us because of the cross? Grace covers the law and the prophets and, with love, fulfills and completes Christ's purpose. Mercy is the noun side of grace, which describes the height of the climb, the character, and posture. Hope describes the verb side, the current of the water, the process, the servant, the work, and the doer, the expectant process. Look at mercy and hope side by side: mercy, or undeserved favor or kindness, is the classic definition of grace; and hope, or divine influence upon the heart, describes how it moves in you. Authority (mercy) is preeminent love judgments in the Godhead, and submission (hope) shows Jesus coming off His throne in obedience. Meekness (mercy) is a state of inward power, and self-control (hope) is your *soul rights* under control. Love (mercy) is mercy before it is acted upon, and joy (hope) is a hopeful inward comeback when love is fulfilled. Gentleness (mercy) is love's touch, self-control is hope's patient posture. Peace (mercy) is the inside referee, and a clear proof of Christ's love in you; and kindness (hope) is hands and feet to a hopeless hurting world.

> You will know them by their fruits.
> —MATTHEW 7:16

The following Scriptures clearly tie hope and grace together:

> Now may our Lord Jesus Christ Himself, and our God and Father, who has loved us and given us everlasting consolation and good hope by grace.
> —2 THESSALONIANS 2:16

> Through whom also we have access by faith into this grace in which we stand, and rejoice in hope of the glory of God.
> —ROMANS 5:2

> Therefore gird up the loins of your mind, be sober, and rest your hope fully upon the grace that is to be brought to you at the revelation of Jesus Christ.
> —1 PETER 1:13

I feel as though I am stuck in a great worship song,

and I do not want to get out. I am sure you can see clearly the threefold chord of hope, grace, and mercy. Passing through the gate of worship is so much fun when you have entered through the throne of grace. What a glorious journey this has been searching out the hope of God. My benediction to you will be from 1 Peter 5:10:

> But may the God of all grace, who called us to His eternal glory by Christ Jesus, after you have suffered [hope] a while, perfect, [hope] establish, [hope] strengthen, [hope] and settle you [hope].

Lord, let us live, and move, and have our being in your blessed hope! *Amen.*

HOPE HIGHLIGHTS

1. Grace, whether its work is to forgive and pardon, to enlighten with knowledge, to declare true judgments, to strengthen in weakness and endurance, or give you gifts and love, is free and without limits.

2. One definition of grace is the divine influence upon the heart.

3. Grace, and hope, and mercy cannot have meaning without Christ's work on the cross. Obedience is our ticket to grace's full benefit. Obedience is to:
   a. Hear and listen attentively;
   b. Obey and respond;
   c. Have a posture of attentiveness; and
   d. Submit everything.

4. Two sides of grace:
   a. Mercy—undeserved kindness, authority, meekness, love acted upon, gentleness, peace.
   b. Hope—divine influence, submission, self-control, joy, longsuffering, kindness.

NOTES

CHAPTER 1
THE ADVERSARIES OF HOPE
1. Oswald Chambers, *My Utmost for His Highest* (Nashville, TN: Thomas Nelson Publishers, 1997).

CHAPTER 3
THE BIRTH OF HOPE—GOD'S PRESENCE
1. Charlotte Baker, *Eye of the Needle: And Other Prophetic Parables* (Hagerstown, MD: McDougal Publishing, 1997). Used by permission.

CHAPTER 4
THE AUTHOR OF HOPE—THE TRINITY
1. James Strong, ed., *Strong's Concordance of the Bible* (Nashville, TN: Thomas Nelson Publishers, 1997), #629.

CHAPTER 6
THE PROGRESSION OF HOPE—THE POTENTIAL OF ONE CALLED FOLLOWER, DISCIPLE, SHEPHERD, KING, PRIEST, APOSTLE
1. Rick Joyner, *The Final Quest* (New Kensington, PA: Whitaker House, 1997), author's paraphrase.

CHAPTER 7
HOPE DEFINED
1. James Strong, ed., *Strong's Concordance of the Bible*, #1680.

CHAPTER 9
HOPE—IT IS ALL ABOUT GRACE

1. James Strong, ed., *Strong's Concordance of the Bible*, #5219.

To contact the author:

Timothy D. Pomp

Tim Pomp
1716 15th St SW
Bemidji, MN 56601

218-750-7333